T0277407

Anything That Moves

JAMIE STEWART

SHEFFIELD – LONDON – NEW YORK

This edition published in 2023 by And Other Stories
Sheffield – London – New York
www.andotherstories.org

3 5 7 9 8 6 4 2

ISBN: 9781913505585
eBook ISBN: 9781913505592

Editor: Jeremy M. Davies; copy-editor: Larissa Melo Pienkowski;
proofreader: Sarah Terry; cover design: Tom Etherington; cover
photography: Jamie Stewart; typeset in Albertan Pro and Syntax by
Tetragon, London. Printed and bound by CPI Limited, Croydon, UK.

And Other Stories gratefully acknowledge that our work is
supported using public funding by Arts Council England.

Dedicated to Thee Dream Fawn

CONTENTS

AUTHOR'S NOTE

If we are related, please, for the love of God, do not read this book.

JOANE CREAMER

My mom had a friend named Joane. She was a few years younger than my mom and had two children with super dumb names, Calamity and Nirvanta. They acted like kids who have dumb names like that act. Joane was pretty and used to come over a lot, wearing a bikini around our house and pool. Once, she, my mom, and all related kids went to the beach a couple days after Joane got a nose job. A Frisbee hit her bandaged-up face and she went unconscious from the pain. The guy who knocked her out was staring at her possibly-dead-but-hot body while my mother screamed "King Pervert!" at him.

When I was around twelve, sometimes I would babysit Joane's children. On the days she drove me home, she would bunch her skirt up to her hips so the beginning of her panties were visible. Any time I looked over, she ran her hands all over her thighs, but she always looked straight ahead at the road.

It didn't bother me, but I wasn't really into it either. Later, when I was in high school, I thought about fucking her—but I also put my dick into a vacuum cleaner hose, so being on THEE FUCK LIST didn't mean much. I know Joane's behavior was something that only a deep-end nutjob would have indulged in, and not that I condone it in any way, but it didn't occur to me then to feel one way or the other about it. To be

11

honest, it doesn't really occur to me to feel anything about it now either. I never thought, *An adult is sort of exposing themself to me!* I remember having a forever-expanding tolerance for people disregarding my feelings when I was a kid; it seemed to happen so often. Today when my feelings are disregarded, I overreact to an avalanchian degree. Energy cannot be created, nor can it disappear, etc.

I'd been checking out porn magazines forever but couldn't figure out how jacking off worked. There would be cartoons with motion lines around someone's cartoon hand and cartoon dick, but I couldn't grasp that you had to keep on doing it for anything to happen. I would jerk it for one or two jerks and be unimpressed. Willing to try anything, I wrapped my cock behind my leg to bend it, squeezed it as hard as I could with two hands, or once and only once rubbed Icy Hot into it, but with no results.

With the theoretical understanding that anal sex existed, I took a butter knife with an oblong bulb at the end of the handle and squatted over my grandmother's antique hand mirror. My sister now has this mirror in her living room. I inserted the knife handle into my butthole and watched it disappear up me in the reflection. It felt like I wanted it to. Suddenly, a spot of cum the size of a dime dripped down onto the mirror.

I went bananas—yanked the knife out and threw it into the bushes. That was the first time my dick did anything other than pee, and it freaked me out. I did not look at porn or touch myself for a couple of months. After I got over it, my mom kept asking everyone why the butter knives kept disappearing and, for some insane reason, I told her.

Faking being at home sick one day and with nothing to do, I went into my parents' room. Under the bed was all the porn I had been fruitlessly investigating. I opened one magazine and put it on the quilted bedspread. It showed a fully aroused penis in a fully aroused vagina. My godmother is a famous quilter and has her work displayed in the Smithsonian. This quilt was one she made.

The coveralls I was wearing—this was during an experimental fashion phase—had open pockets, so you could put your hands all the way inside without unzipping the front. Finally, of its own instinctual, wanting accord, my hand, as if it were The Hand itself, spider crawled inside of my coveralls and began jerking and jerking without stopping. I turned the pages with my other free hand and kept working, totally focused on the pictures and not totally conscious of what else was happening

Violently, confusedly, and opulently, I ejaculated. It felt yellowy and thick. Looking up, I saw Joane standing well inside the doorway of my parents' room. She had watched me cum for my first time. I noticed her hair had been dyed from blond to black. She'd showed up to borrow something from my mom, I guessed. We stared at each other.

My hand was still inside the open pocket, and the porn magazine was still on the bed. She walked out of the room and started looking around the house for whatever it was she needed. It took her a very long time to find it. I stayed frozen and could feel the cum on my underpants clogging up. Lamely, I have maintained a grinding preference for black hair my entire life. Also, if you haven't caught this already, Joane's last name was Creamer.

GAVIN ENGELBERG

My mom and dad had a lot of emotional and psychological problems, and they were very young when they had me. There probably wasn't as much supervision as there should have been. When I was eight or nine, I played with twin brothers named Gavin and Reuben. They were Guatemalan and had been adopted by our white, Jewish neighbors. The husband was a nephrologist and the wife was a well-known autism specialist. Later, the husband was accidentally electrocuted and died, and after his death, the wife used to talk to my mom about jerking herself off with gradually larger and larger vegetables.

On good days, the lack of supervision was a marvel in that it led to free, long-form adventures I can't imagine any kids I know having now. But on bad days, it was only debilitating and led to a feeling of being permanently unsafe, day or night.

Gavin and Reuben were bonkers, and they wanted to do every dangerous and upsetting thing they could think of. They played with firecrackers, motor oil, a real bow and arrow, and BB guns; lit a palm tree on fire; smoked dead bees wrapped in dried leaves; buried each other up to the neck in rocks and dirt; and climbed to the tops of telephone poles. I was shy and frightened of everything and would only stand by, half sobbing, as they rode further and further into the Children's Chaos.

When they were older, they once purposely crashed their grandmother's Cadillac into an Andy Gump port-a-potty that was in a park on the edge of a baseball diamond. It flew into the air and landed on the roof of the car, which shattered the windshield. Sixty gallons of hot, rotting Little League sewage dumped all over them, filling the car. They were drenched and screaming through the endless dark curtain.

Even though they were eternally bent on killing themselves, Gavin saved my life once. My parents tied a hangman's noose in our avocado tree for a Halloween party. It stayed in the tree for months. When I was outside playing with Gavin, I stood on a bucket with my hands under my chin and threaded my head into the noose. I kicked the bucket away, thinking I could just pull my head out. It became immediately clear I had no air and could not get free. Gavin was on the other side of the yard with his back to me, playing on the ground with bugs. By chance, he turned and rushed over to put the bucket back under my feet. We knew I had almost died and he held both my hands like a vicar until I calmed down.

Gavin, Reuben, and I were obsessed with fantasy and sword worlds and role-playing games like Dungeons & Dragons. We played every day, and the dice and paper games morphed into the clunkily dubbed "D&D: We Are the Characters," meaning, we ran all around the neighborhood with hatchets, long screwdrivers, PVC pipes, and trash can-lid shields. We spent weeks creating the details of our fantastical selves within the games. To be cruel to one another, we would sometimes throw the pieces of paper that our characters were recorded onto into Gavin and Reuben's pool. It always made someone cry.

As an offshoot of D&D, we were also into Greek mythology, unicorns, and Pegasus. Gavin had a collection of unicorn plush toys; Reuben had a collection of Pegasus plush toys. Although both boys were physically intense, they were also very sensitive, and in exasperated submission to these sensitivities, their parents basically let them do whatever they wanted. The combination of no rules, no adults around, big imaginations, and big emotions led to Gavin falling in love with one of his unicorn dolls. Its name was Merganzer. Reuben and I were merciless when we found out and pinched and slapped Merganzer in the face. Gavin wailed with such genuine sadness that it shocked us into stopping. He didn't talk to us for days. To try and cheer him up, we would dig little holes, fill them with dry pine needles, tie plastic Smurf figures to sticks we shoved into the dirt, and light them on fire as melting sacrifices to Hera, Zeus, and Poseidon.

One night, I was sleeping over, Reuben was at a friend's house, and their mom and dad were out for the evening. There was no babysitter. Gavin said, "I need you to do something for me. I need you to take photos of me making love to my unicorn."

"Which one?" I asked, though of course I knew.

"Merganzer," he whispered. He handed me a Polaroid camera and took off his clothes. I stood in the corner, watching and holding the camera like it was a cake I had dropped and then picked up off the floor.

The previous winter, I had stolen a small, two-blade Swiss Army knife from my dad's bureau. I dropped it in a gutter during a rainstorm and pretended I found it there. Gavin saw me drop it in. He shook his head in trifling disgust and grabbed it away from me. Using this knife now, he poked a tiny hole in the seam along the doll's rump. He had a little boy's erection and got behind the unicorn, inserting himself into the hole. He began to pump.

On his raw, dark pink butthole, which would flash open each time he reared back for a thrust, there was a perfectly round, heavy, chocolate donut of his shit. Gavin explained to me months before that he could not wipe his ass anymore because witches lived up in there. He was afraid they would grab his fingers and pull him inside himself. I pictured one inside him, standing on a little raft and pushing herself along with an enchanted staff.

"Merganzer, Merganzer . . . " he moaned.

I took nine photos quickly. The Polaroids fell from the camera onto the carpet as their images came to life. Gavin gathered them to his breast like novenas and peered down into the stack as if for some holy response. He no longer seemed to be aware of me. I told him I was scared and was going to go home. I only lived a couple of houses away but usually got anxious during sleepovers, so he was used to me leaving suddenly. I ran across the street and across the lawn of our quietly mean, uptight Canadian neighbors and saw that someone had left a dead rat on the hood of their Mercedes.

LAMONTE

When I was a child, my dad would deposit me into a network of children's corrals with the other offspring of the musicians he worked with. It made sense: stoned dads dropping their underdeveloped hippie-funk mistakes off at someone's back-yard or big house to run around and police themselves while they made records, hung out, and took drugs.

Two of the kids in this network I knew were a girl named Nala and her brother Lamonte. Once, those two; my sister; our next-door neighbor, Kevin Jeong; and I were sitting in a car in a parking lot with no grown-ups around. My dad left us in there to go do something. We were getting tired of waiting, so I suggested that when we got back to my house, all the boys should put each other's dicks into each other's butts and make a circle. In the middle of the circle, there would be a bonfire. We could triple howl and dance around its flickering hobbit flame. Bending my arms at an unnatural angle, I started to demonstrate what the vibe of this dance might be. My sister and Nala started screaming in amused horror, which then inspired Lamonte, Kevin, and I to start screaming in amused delight. So then, locked alone in a car in a parking lot, were five screaming children. A security guard or some other reasonable citizen must have eventually found my dad because he came running over with a terrified-and-then-relieved look on his face. He tried to explain to us how frightening our behavior might seem to strangers and exhorted us not to do it, but we just kept screaming and grinning while he tried to get us to cool it.

The next day, I was at Nala and Lamonte's. We were very little. Nala was maybe four, Lamonte six, and I was maybe five? At that time, it was popular to make rubber erasers in the shapes of animals, buses, people, or fruit. Nala had a collection of presidential bust erasers. They were all gray, about the size of a prune, and must have come in a set. We were seeing what it was like to stuff as many as we could into our mouths. They were very detailed and crevice-y, so our spit collected in them and would pour out all over us when we pulled them out again.

Lamonte imperiously told Nala to get out of her own room, which made her cry. She stomped away. He told me we should climb into his tree house and do what we'd talked about the day before in the car. The tree house was not really in a tree but more a part of a jungle gym that had a little Lincoln Log shack on top. Next to it was a picnic table where we (or Lamonte's mother) had made us SpaghettiOs for breakfast. The ones we'd spilled were now hardened in yellow and red on the table, a constellation of smaller Os baked by the sun inside a constellation of bigger Os.

We climbed up the ladder and it seemed very high but couldn't have been more than six or seven feet up, because I remember on another day someone's dad handing us up binoculars to play with. When we got up there, Lamonte very quickly took off his clothes and started a bouncing syncopated chant, "I'm gonna strip . . . (cha cha cha), I'm gonna strip . . . "

His back was curved in and his belly button poked out like half a Superball. It looked like someone should probably draw some eyes and a frown around it and turn it into a depressing cartoon. His penis was bucking in time with his song, and he began to walk in a circle, smiling and laughing. I was all for it but nervous, so I just pulled my pants down. I was wearing a plaid collared shirt and a V-neck sweater. He approached me from behind, and I had to hold up my shirttails to expose my hole.

When his dick went inside, I remember it being very easy, and the sensation was something I couldn't then describe. I neither liked it nor disliked it; I just didn't know. Lamonte was giggling, making funny duck sounds so it made everything seem silly, which it was. He didn't thrust in and out but just kept it in and kept his chant and springy rhythm going.

After a little bit, he pulled himself out. We got dressed and felt super wild and out of control but in a fun way. He and I started jumping out of the window of the tree house and onto the dirt and grass and climbing back in and doing it over and over again. I felt like we repeated the jump a hundred thousand times. Somehow, our unfinished skeletons remained indestructible inside us, but our clothes were filthy by the time we ran out of this rampaging, entangled energy.

Late that night, my mom picked me up. My dad stayed where he was to keep playing music. There was a clock from Las Vegas on the wall and its numbers were dice. One of my parents had cut out simple Arabic numerals and taped them to the dice so I could learn to tell time. So I know it was around 11 p.m. when we got home.

I sat on the rug, and my mom sat on the couch. My sister was asleep in a child-sized, black-and-orange rocking chair that had chess piece-shaped decorations carved into it. When I sat down, I could still feel a clear ghost of pressure from Lamonte's dick in my butthole. When I stood, it was gone; when I sat, it returned. It was an interesting sensation. I kept standing and sitting.

My mom asked me what I was doing. I told her that I had done something that I wasn't sure I should have done. She put her face up to my face and asked what it was. A voice came into my head that told me that, for everyone's sake, I should not, under any circumstances, explain things. This voice has continued to rescue me from execution my entire life. I told her I didn't want to say. The sensation in my butt was pulsing. She glared at me for a moment and then went into her room and closed the door.

A few months later, my parents accidentally woke me up in the middle of the night while they were checking my butthole for worms with a flashlight. I wanted to keep my mouth shut about it, but in the morning, I was too worried and nervously asked my mom what was going on the night before. The answer was strange and gross, but it was a relief, as I had assumed she'd somehow figured out what I did with Lamonte and was looking for proof of all that I had been quietly feeling.

DOTTY CISNEROS

For a while, I went to a tiny school with about twenty-five students per grade. The kids all stayed at their desks and the teachers changed rooms for each subject. Almost everyone there started in kindergarten, so they'd grown up together and were intensely territorial. I started in the fifth grade and was teased mercilessly the entire year for saying the word *like* a lot, for parting my hair in the middle, and for only wearing black, iron-on, movie-monster T-shirts. I cried to my parents, and they answered in the way they often did, with a rousing, "Life isn't fair." In some ways, their motto made me more realistic and self-reliant, and in some ways, it made me callous and viciously self-preservatory. The meanest girl in class—with whom I would later share my first kiss underwater at a pool party, and with whose older brother my sister would unhappily lose her virginity—called me "Rainbow Man" relentlessly, like a hundred times a day and for reasons I have never understood. She had a flat, turned-up pig nose, and the brother had a pig nose too. His unachieved goal in life was to manage a Fatburger in the Valley. She now works as a bank manager on the Death Star.

The next year, I wasn't fresh fruit anymore and therefore was obliged to terrorize the next new kid. As a class, we managed to run off at least one incoming student per semester—one for being a hesher, one for having what we decided was a Russian accent, one for wearing a pelvic brace as a result of having survived a near-fatal car accident, and, as if we were all the low-foreheaded employees of some small-town meat-packing plant in the 1950s, one for dressing fashionably. On and on the breaking wheel must spin!

Dotty started in the eighth grade, the last grade that school offered. She was the tallest person in the class, which saved her from being hassled by the feckless boys, but she was the most physically developed, which meant the trendy girls gave her a ton of shit. Half the class was obsessed with her but afraid of her powerful grip, and half the class wanted to be her but was threatened by her vast puberty.

She seemed to float above the hand-wringing mayhem of the court. Some days she read by herself under a tree, some days she hung out with the nerd girls and traded *Robotech* comics, and some days she played basketball with the couple jock boys and took their five-dollar sunglasses if they lost. From what I could tell, she wasn't openly messing around with anyone in our school, though there weren't that many of us and we had all already made out with everyone else, so what would it have mattered. I assumed she must have had an older someone at another school. We didn't talk much.

Our lockers were inside our classrooms; mine was a lower one, behind the teacher's desk. I was starting to get really into music at this point, trying to be an art fag, and was crouched down, taping a magazine page of David Byrne onto the inside of my locker door. Dotty slid up and faced me with her knees against my knees.

She said, "I'm going to show you my tits," and unbuttoned her shirt. Her bra was lace, unpadded, front-clipped with no underwire, and neon yellow. Her skin was dark brown, and the bra was magnificently bright against it. My mind turned to sand. She was beginning to unfasten the clip when, suddenly, she snapped her shirt closed hard.

Looming over us was Mrs. Spanns. She was the strictest and most uptight of our teachers. A no-hand-holding rule had just been enacted at the school, so this bra thing was explosively unallowed. Mrs. Spanns asked what we were doing, and Dotty, without looking up and in a totally uncool, excessive French accent said, "Using our heads talking about Talking Heads." It was obvious she was holding her unbuttoned shirt closed, but I think Mrs. Spanns knew she wouldn't be able to handle that much complication in jelly. After breathing on us for a minute, she walked away.

From where my desk was assigned in her class, I had a view out of a narrow window that I guess would have been used for ventilation before there was central cooling. It had a metal screen over it to keep it from being broken by rocks, I assumed, because it was too small for anyone to fit through. Mostly I was a good student, not because I cared about school but because things were so disordered at home, it was something solid to hold onto. That said, I was taken to long periods of not paying attention, staring out that window at the crisscrossed blue sky. I was preoccupied with thoughts of someone I loved being killed in an earthquake by a collapsed building and my pulling their body out of the pulverized concrete by their arm. Every night now still looking for something solid to hold onto, I pray this prayer,

24

"Jesus Christ, in your most holy name, please prevent a medium or big earthquake from affecting any populated place in the universe."

After our behind-the-locker thing, Dotty and I started saying hi everyday but, other than that, didn't talk any more than we had before. The class was going to take its traditional end-of-the-year retreat to the circularly named Camp YoliJwa Lutheran Camp. After we got there, Dotty told me that she wanted to go on a walk alone with me. She looked into my face, a coquelicot-and-black-glitter nimbus around her, and smiled.

There was a lot of free time, but boys and girls weren't supposed to go into the woods alone, so, as a boy and girl alone, we discussed that we had to be quiet about it—and slick. We were confident we could handle the escape, but it was even easier than we thought it would be. There was not an adult in sight. My sister later became a teacher and took her students to that same camp and told me that all the teachers drank boxed wine the entire time, so it makes sense.

We walked for a little while—not far but far enough—and straddled a mossy log, facing each other. Even though it was almost summer, it was pretty cold, and we were wearing pants instead of shorts so the bark didn't bug us.

We started to kiss. I had made out a few times before and had once licked Shasta Wilmont's boobs. Shasta and I had been laying on the beach, and I pulled off her shirt and bra and went for it. The waves came and drenched us, and people could see everything we were doing. I thought it would be like a cool music video, but it was freezing and sand got up in everything. Several people walked by us, baldly staring.

Our tableau, Shasta later told me, was above and beyond agonizing, and she retreated from any further confidences.

Dotty, however, seemed above and beyond comfortable with what might happen, and into it. She placed both her hands on my thighs.

"I want to see your dick, and I want us to fuck."

My field of vision went all pale. I'd never heard anyone say the F-word out loud in this context and mean it. I told her that I wanted to wait until I was in love with someone. I have no idea if I really felt this way, but the part of getting really into music was also trying to be excessively romantic. I once walked down Nordhoff Street wearing no shoes, no shirt, and a beret. I was holding a red rose and had a small pewter stallion in my blue jeans pocket that I had painted gray with a pedestal of green grass. I planned to give them to the first cute person I saw. No one came along, so, with a great flourish, I cast my heavenly rose into the street and watched cars run it over.

She said, "But all guys want it."

I said, "I don't want to be like all guys."

Again, I am not sure if I meant this, if I was just scared, or if I was trying to develop an irredeemable, "painterly" identity. I do clearly remember saying this, though, and it makes me want to hold my fourteen-year-old self facedown in the mud.

She looked away and said that it was OK. We sat on the log and talked some more and kissed a little more. We were in the forest, so there were birds singing over our heads. They draped pink and blue ribbons around our shoulders. A toad wearing a waistcoat and monocle rolled up to us, driving a tomato with rubber wheels. He pulled out his pocket watch and croaked at us wildly that we were late for our next Bible study.

We graduated and never saw each other again, but we did call each other a few times. During the summer, she sent me a card. Before I could read it, my mom took it. She was in the habit of prying open my personal development. She read my diary, listened in on the other line when I was on the phone, took secret passed-in-class notes out of my book bag, and, as here, read my mail. She and my dad would make fun of me for what I would say and write to people. Once, I guess they saw me kissing someone when I didn't know it and mockingly acted out how I behaved and what I'd looked like while I did it. Until I was in my late thirties, I had to concentrate to get my parents out of my head while I was having sex, but there were a lot of other shitty reasons for that too.

My mom shrieked, "Who sent you this?"

The card had a cartoon chola dressed in booty shorts and a bikini top on the front with a big smile on her face, and it said, "Do you have a license to carry that weapon?" On the inside was a cartoon bull with a smirk on his face, and, in red marker:

XOXOXOXO Thee Miss Dotty Cisneros!

My mom was real tweaked and I didn't want to risk the guaranteed ridicule by explaining everything, so I told her it was just a friend being funny, which was true.

Thinking of Shasta, before making out with her on the beach, it never occurred to me that someone might not like doing something sexual with the person they were dating. That I made her feel bad shook me up, deeply but very slowly. Gradually, I became more and more passive and even regressively against being physically forward with anyone I was going with. In high school, I was broken up with twice for being too demure, and other than Shasta and despite Dotty's best efforts, I didn't see another real human boob until I was eighteen.

BERNARD CYRUS LAMAR

Bernard was born in Louisiana in 1921, so obviously he was a horrible person. Bernard was called Gramps, and now my sister's kids call my mom's nice husband Gramps to perhaps cleanse us of all unrighteousness. Bernard, who with everyone but his grandchildren went by the transformative "Beau," was queer in a time and from a place when that wasn't something anyone could manage. To get away, he took diction classes to erase his accent, earned three master's degrees related to maritime pursuits, and became a sailor and then captain of merchant marine ships in the Pacific Rim. When my mother was a child, he was at sea for months and then usually only home for a couple of days between transport missions. When he returned, he often brought different women with him, for whom my grandmother was expected to make dinner. It seemed like something one would do who was trying hard to appear different from what he was. This violent ejection away from how and where God made him violently shaped my mother, who, in turn, violently shaped me.

When Bernard was younger, from the photos I've seen, he was a stone-cold dandy: in uniform, on deck, his arm around a cabin boy, in a tailored, wide-lapel, three-piece suit and cravat, beyond dashing and beyond handsome, his hair a flawless dream. Even when I was little, I could see how infuriated, curt, and hostile he was to everyone else, but he was never unkind to me. I think he could tell I was like him.

His house was in Sausalito and filled with museum-quality antique ceramics, cinnabar jewelry boxes, gilt furniture, and wood-block prints from China, Japan, the Philippines, and Melanesia. In exchange for smuggling people from Asia to California, he'd asked to be paid in antiques instead of cash. My mother has slowly been giving them to me, and now my house looks almost as criminally beautiful as his.

Her brother, Uncle Vincent, would steal these antiques from my grandmother, mom, and me whenever he could. He pawned them presumably for drugs or just out of spite, for we never saw them in his own house. And though he grew up in that effete and affluent Bay Area home, he became the bizarro-world version of his father. He affected a Southern accent, which he would have never heard from anyone around him, for his father's had been deleted before he was born; became a speed-freak long-haul truck driver, moved to Indiana, and put entire sheets of acid into the gas tank of his motorcycle so his bike could trip with him. How do I know this? Because when he was babysitting, he told me, and then later that day chased me up a grapefruit tree that he then shook until I fell to the ground, breaking my nose. He also seemed to have goats around him like butterflies. He vanished after faking his death to avoid paying taxes. A cousin wrote me eight years later to say he finally, actually died. I hesitated to tell my mother—why befuddle her grief? But my sister, who has kids and a more normal sense of what a family ought to be, told me I should. My mom cried and cried and cried.

There's no way on earth or in hell that I can or am going to slog through the details ever again of my mother abusing me. I'm done with it. Our relationship is new, she is new, and life is already cruel enough to forgo the peace of forgiveness. But when I first was finally able to talk to her about it, she tried to explain maybe why or how—though not in an attempt to excuse what she did. She revealed to me that her father, Bernard, her brother Vincent; and her brother Leonard, about whom the only other things I know are that he died young riding a bicycle and that he killed my grandma's canaries with a hose; had savagely and relentlessly abused *her*. My mother's fingers are crooked from them having broken them; she still walks with a slight limp and has had tinnitus since she was a child from repeated head trauma. That was her life until she moved out at age sixteen to open a flower shop called Blooms and Growths.

My mother's tears were so confused when I told her that Vincent had died again. To her remarkable credit, she told me that what hurt most was that she wished she had known he was alive to have been able to try and mend their hearts back together. They were children when all the awful things happened. I understood then that she was so young when she had me, barely twenty, that she was almost a child when she hurt me too.

On my dresser is a remarkably lovely set of seventeenth-century Japanese bowls. They were a payment to my grandpa, then given to my mother and now to me. I never ever think about what else happened when I look at them.

During my last semester of college, I went to visit Bernard when he was dying. It was my first time seeing him in years; we'd been banned from visiting after my father borrowed money from him and didn't pay him back. He was sunken into the squishy, brown BarcaLounger he always sat in, but he was covered in a thin layer of white talc, extra gaunt, totally hairless, and, oddly, super chatty. He was a hard drinker and I never recall him not having a pint glass filled with ice and straight vodka in his hand. But it made him a quiet and grim reaper. I would always eat the bitter ice cubes out of the glass when it was empty and then refill it with two hands from the giant bottle in the freezer.

I thought I should try and find out as much about him as I could, now or never. My mother grew up under the impression that his mother, Vera May, was a Pawnee Indian. I asked him to tell me about her and what he knew about her childhood. He started cackling and pointed at me like I was a dunce. He said that he made the whole thing up— his mother was white. My mother had gone her whole life thinking she was a quarter Indigenous American and told me I was an eighth Indigenous American. Under the advisement of a guidance counselor, I even put it on my college application and was invited to join the Native American Student Scholarship Association at SFSU. I never went, but I got mail from them for years afterward. When I told my mom he had lied to her, she cursed him a defeated curse and smashed a coffee cup in the sink. She gathered up the disappointed shards in her bare hands and threw them on the street. Little blood drops made a trail to her slammed bedroom door.

That day, Bernard told me that there was something he wanted me to have. In the hall closet was a massive 1960s reel-to-reel Sony tape machine that was so heavy I wasn't sure I could carry it into my car. There were also about a hundred flat boxes of quarter-inch tapes. He said that he'd had them on his ship. I was so excited, thinking that maybe the tapes were his journals. He held my hand and told me it was very important to him that I listen to them right away. I felt very special that he was opening his life to me.

The next time I saw him was in the hospital only a couple weeks later. He looked like a translucent apple core. I started to cry, and he patted my wrist weakly while ghost wind came out of his mouth. His eyes were dark gray buttons. I was so relieved and sad when the nurse told me I had to leave. In the middle of the night, I woke up and could feel he was dead.

None of the tapes were labeled. The first one I played was the soundtrack to *Kiss Me, Kate*. The next was the soundtrack to *Seven Brides for Seven Brothers*. The next one was the soundtrack to *South Pacific*. All of the hundred tapes—except for one, which was the Harmonicats—were fucking show tunes and musicals. He was telling me he was a queen. I brought this up to my mother. It upset her and she didn't want to hear it.

A couple of months before, while I was out with a friend in San Francisco, I lost my car keys. I called my mother on a pay phone to ask if she could bring me my other set. When she arrived, she threw the keys at my chest, spat at me, and screamed in my face, "I hate that you're gay!" (Although I am and always have been bi- or pan- or whatever; see the title of the book in your hands.) To get back at her, I absolutely reveled in taunting her with the details of my deductions: her father's overly visible mistresses, his way-too-nice clothes, his cabin-boy photos, his being a sailor in the first place, his antiques, and, the most compelling evidence, the tapes. My mother put her hands over her ears and yelled, "Shut up! Shut up!" On a long car ride, she finally asked her mom if it was true. My grandma looked out the window and replied in a high, shriveled voice, "Coulda been." My siblings and I thought this was hilarious. They don't know about what my mother's father and brothers did to her, and they don't know what she did to me.

My brother named his son Bernard. I wanted to tell him he shouldn't, but I couldn't tell him why. My mom knew that this was what he was going to name his son, and she knew he was doing it because he thought it would make her happy. My nephew Bernard could be my grandfather's spirit being given another chance to do the right thing, and I hope he chooses that path. He has a lot pulling him in other directions, but I have faith in his heart. I have never asked my mom how she feels about my nephew's name, and I don't think I ever will. Her father has taken up enough space in her life already.

JUANA COVARRUBIAS

She was the first real girlfriend I had and the first person that, in a tolerant retrospect, I was in love with. We met at an open mic where my "piece" was to shave one of my armpits and then read from an outdated nautical service manual. It was, even in a tolerant retrospect, stupid. After we dated for a while, I got her nickname tattooed on my shoulder and she had my nickname tattooed on her thigh, but I would guess that she has—as I have—probably covered it up by now. When I got her number, she was with her sisters, of whom she was number two out of four, and she talked to me in a comical Brooklyn accent. Her real accent was Valley Girl Chicana, so the "hey Tony" thing was funny.

Juana was a virgin when we started dating, and I was almost a virgin. Even so, she was adventurous and creative, much more than I was. She told me that on the night she was going to lose it, she wanted to shave my entire body. This sounded terrible to me, but getting laid sounded rad, so I said OK.

Her parents were Catholic Fascists, so there was no way we could do it at her house, although later, she found that the risk of getting caught turned her on and we would fuck in the living room while the rest of her entire family were playing cards in the dining room ten feet away.

As a testament to how gross I was, I suggested that we could do it in my mom's bed. My parents were separated, so my dad wasn't around, though they did get back together a couple of years later. I knew when my mom would be out of town visiting him, so we planned it for then. I kept hoping Juana would forget about the shaving thing, but when she came over, she waved about four cheap, white, single-blade disposable razors like willing teen mystical wands.

We stood in the shower and she soaped me up. She started with my chest and armpits, which were easy. Then she did my pubes, but we didn't know how to shave my balls, so the effort looked unbalanced. She wanted to do my stomach but it wasn't that fuzzy, so I thought if she shaved there it would come back in too thick. She was cool about it and compromised. By this time, there was a lot of hair in the drain, and the crappy razors had gotten quite dull. I was not looking forward to my legs and refused my arms. My head was already cut in a buzz so, close enough. I knew I would get fired from my job if she shaved my eyebrows, but she wanted to.

The razors were excruciating when she started on my legs and there was no more hot water left. This servility took about forty-five minutes and I looked, with my farmer tan, like a Creamsicle Neapolitan freak. For some reason, she still wanted to fuck me. It proceeded as dumbly as expected. We didn't know about lube, so cramming my dry condom dick into her dry, nervous pussy made it feel like a trash fire. I tried to go gently, but she got impatient and snapped at me to just push it in. I hoped it would be beautiful and she hoped to get it over with. She cried a little afterward. I took her home, and when, under the starlight, I asked her how she felt, she just told me it hurt. So then I started crying and she got mad. It was a super sexy night.

Her older sister, Panfila, was going to USC, and for some reason Juana invited me to meet them there the next day. She didn't say where. USC is a big place, and it took us about an hour to find each other. My entire body was infested with shaving bumps. I looked like every bee on earth had a tiny spear gun and shot me with it and then also stung me. It SUCKED. Juana told me again how much her vagina hurt, so I didn't complain too much. When my mom came back, she was furious we had clogged up the shower drain. I explained how it happened, which I thought would be a sound justification. When I think now about all the wrong, wrong, wrong things I told my mom, I put my head in my hands. Then I think of all the wrong, wrong, wrong things she told me, and I put my head in my hands again.

Juana and I kept banging and figured it out a little more each time. We were pretty compatible in how willing we both were to try new things. I "borrowed" sex books from the bookstore I worked at and we looked through them together. It was fun. She tried to be fun, generally. We made little driftwood huts at the beach, took our first road trip together in a car *she fucking stole* (and then returned), went to museums a lot, fucked in weird places, things like that. She helped me to be less boring.

A couple of months after the first time we slept together, my mom moved to another house. I hadn't gotten my act together, so I moved with her. I was kind of a loser and

I moved in and out of my parents' houses until I was way too old to be doing that kind of thing. Juana and I conducted deeper and further explorations over the seven seas of jizz all across my adult bedroom, in my adult mom's rented house in the Valley. It had peach walls and peach carpet.

In one of the sex books, there was a part about rimming, and we didn't really understand it at first. But from a design perspective, the words *oral* and *anal* look good on a page together, so we wanted to know. She put her tongue on my butthole and it felt unbelievable. I did it to her and she had the same reaction.

It became one of our main things. Even though she was still technically a teenager, I have never been with anyone since—even men—who liked rimming so much. This girl fucking loved to eat ass and have her ass eaten. Close to a year into our relationship, I was going around up in there and I felt a little something on my tongue. My internal reaction was, *OK, it was bound to happen, there is a little piece of shit. This is very yucky, but whatever. I will use mouthwash like Divine in* Pink Flamingos.

I wiped my tongue off on the back of my hand and it was a tapeworm. I had licked a tapeworm out of her ass. I brushed the worm off onto the side of the mattress and moved on to other things. My mind froze in shock. I never told her.

It was great for a long time; however, as we got closer, it started to feel like she had a gradual, crawling, sort of stultifyingly off-the-mark personality, and, being young and a dope, I didn't know how to deal with it anymore. It was stultifying to me because it was so hard to know if the "capers" (this was her favorite word) she organized were genuinely exciting and subversive or just clownish, and there was no way to try and talk that out without being insulting.

She did stuff like asking me to come and play free jazz upright bass, which I could not do, at her high school talent show, while she and her sister sat on the edge of the stage and incanted a very slow slam poetry version of "The Mercy Seat" by Nick Cave and the Bad Seeds, not as a joke. It took about ten minutes to get through. On one hand, *maybe* this was actually sort of a cool thing to do at a high school talent show in Newhall because it was totally, totally strange, but on the other hand, I bet it sounded incredibly bad and *maybe* it was just a poorly thought-out, unnecessary imposition of lunatic grandiosity in an entirely incorrect context—if there is a conceivably correct context for this? I felt super embarrassed doing it but was excited to play at all, if quite badly, in front of people. That was kind of her vibe: possibly ultra-fearless enthusiasm but also very possibly cringe-inducing miscalculation. It became difficult to know how to feel about her, and this difficult feeling became a puzzling burden to me.

Eventually it was too confusing a burden and I broke up with her over the phone, more or less out of the blue. When she rightly demanded, through tears, to know why I said something like, "A switch flipped off in my mind like it was slowly filled with a dark matter of distance I could not name." That must have been awesome for her. I have blundered my way through many of my own cringe-inducing miscalculations during other breakups, but that one . . . Mamma mia.

We stayed in very loose touch after our breakup, and later she told me she realized she was a dyke. When we were still dating, we both came out to each other as bi. It was really hard for her. Without my asking, she then said it was eating so much ass that eventually made it clear she was a lesbian. I wasn't entirely sure how this added up and didn't want to be disrespectful so didn't ask, *You mean because it's kind of closer to eating pussy than sucking a cock?* But I was thinking it. I just said, "Congratulations."

ZOOEY ZUCCARELI

When I was going to community college, I dated a really cool but cuckoo-bananas woman named Tonya for a couple of months. She dyed her hair silvery gray and wore a kind of *World According to Garp* fuzzy-bear costume without the bear head all the time. She would dye her pubic and butthole hair silvery gray also, and when I went down on her, I could see she had silvery, caked-up dingleberries.

I was never too serious about her, but it was more or less enjoyable. Tonya was absolutely emphatic about things being fair, though: who drove to whose house last time, who called more often, whose turn it was to end the good-night hug first, who lit more incense at the temple of obsessive reciprocation, etc. I was not as attentive to this—or her, really—as I could have been. When she called to break up with me, I was in the bathroom, taking a shit. I could not help myself and said, "Hey, I am taking a dump while I am getting dumped." She was incredibly pissed. This was, for reasons other than inhumanity, poorly considered because I already knew she wasn't one to fuck around when she made enemies. When she got fired from her job at Conrad's, which was a high-end collectible-doll boutique, she kept her key and came back at night to light the office on fire. Shelf after shelf of four-hundred-dollar little bodies, little dresses, and little wigs, turned to ash. The dolls mostly had ceramic heads with glass eyes. Ceramic doesn't burn, but glass melts, so littered about the carbonized debris were hundreds of cheerful or coy eyeless and stark-white children's faces. Her friend Zooey, who Tonya fucked once, told me about all this. Not long after Tonya gave me the boot, Zooey and I started going out.

Zooey was a made-up name; she was actually named Naomi and tried to work in the Bay Area as a dominatrix at a time when there were already way too many of them. She spoke in an overly modulated voice and she was always *on*. Her apartment was old without having any character; unusually small and stuffed into it somewhere was a seven-year-old daughter. Zooey liked anal more than vaginal sex and liked to have her nipples bitten so deeply I was genuinely afraid I was going to tear one off. She told me to pull her hair harder, harder, harder and, after I came, would tell me I was sick in an accusing, virtuous tone.

I started playing little pickup funk or dub shows in empty bars and would be done after 2 a.m. She said this was a good time to come over because her child would be asleep. One night when I showed up, she was sitting on her couch and pushing a piece of piercing jewelry up into her urethra until it poked out of the flesh above it. I saw the chrome pop out through the pink. Then she took one of her daughter's action figures and slipped it into her vagina. Then she took another one of her daughter's action figures and slipped that up her vagina too. She lay on her back on the cushions, and there was a little trickle of blood coming down from the hole she had poked in herself. With a big grin on her face and as she contracted her muscles, the action figures shot out. We started to see more and more of each other.

I was very young and very lost, and my subconscious was beginning to work through the festering crack of what was my childhood. About a month into our dating, Zooey took me on a short camping trip, and while we were in a little tent by a creek she told me she loved me. I started to try and say that I wanted to feel that also but it was still too new, but before I could start, she placed a finger over my lips to shush me. Earlier on the drive, she also told me she needed a new apartment because she was getting evicted. She needed someone to split the rent and someone upon whom a credit check could be "successfully committed." I would have done anything anyone asked me. A week later, we moved in together. In her tiny, nondescript mom car on the drive back from camping, she told me she loved the road and could feel it coming through her body.

Through the play scene, she had a connection to a very famous modern primitive originator . . . His partner had been Zooey's dom, then her mistress, and then BDSM instructor. Zooey took me to a party at their super-everyday house in San Bruno. It was a funny scene. There were only a few people who were full-on done up in leather gear and costumes, but mostly people were wearing cargo shorts and wraparound sunglasses. Everyone was friendly enough, though. Zooey took me on a quick tour of the house, and in the bedroom there was a fuck sling filled with teddy bears and stuffed penguins. Hung on pegs in a tight grid, totally covering one of the walls floor-to-ceiling, were vintage Halloween masks. Being around the people who actually did what she could only want to do made Zooey anxious to try and impress them. She buzzed around everyone, ignoring me. I moped around the house, not knowing anyone there, and in order to be anywhere but there, I looked at the travel photo books on the coffee table.

After I fell asleep in a chair in the living room, Zooey woke me up by snapping her fingers in my face. She was holding a bongo and wearing a batik skirt, and she was naked from the waist up. For a second, I felt less tired, until she led me to the backyard, where she wanted me to play this bongo while she did a dumb serpent dance. People made an uncomfortable circle around her, holding beers and bags of Cheetos. She was trying to get her accomplished hosts to engage in her dance, but they were in other conversations and just gave her weak mano cornuto signs or kind of waved at her once in a while.

She was bristling and frenzied when we got back to the cheap stucco duplex we'd just moved into. Her daughter was at Zooey's *horrendous* walleyed mother's house while we finished setting the place up. She pulled me by the arm into the bathroom and showed me what a speculum was. She turned the screw to open herself up and told me to get on my knees and look inside. I saw an IUD string hanging out of her cervix. It looked like a soft penis head with a zip tie coming out of the urethra, and I didn't know what it was, so I asked her if it was an S&M thing. She duck walked with it still inside her to the mattress on the floor of our room. Lying on her back, she rubbed her clit, shrieked, then yanked the speculum out. While I stared in amazement, she whimpered in a baby-talk voice that she wanted to teach me how to fist her. When I was in her to the wrist, she told me she knew that

I wanted to push my cock inside too. I opened my hand as much as it would, slid into my palm, and jacked myself while all the way up her. Her eyes rolled around in crazy ways, but she was totally silent.

The next morning, she was walking around the couple of rooms in circles and asked me if I wanted to be wrapped up in cellophane. I wanted to say yes to what life had to offer and have her think I was a good boy. She got it out and very quickly I was immobilized. She said over and over again that she could stab me anytime she wanted to. She took a kitchen knife and ran it all over my wrapping. My mind turned off and I didn't feel anything. Lately, she'd complain—regardless of where we were or what we were doing—that I never came when she gave me blow jobs. She would snort again and again in irritation, "What's wrong with you?" Resplendent in ego and insecurity, she'd started to withhold giving me head. Now she cut a slit around my cock with the knife, pulled it out, and began to lick it.

When I was hard, she lit two sticks of incense and flicked them near and around my shaft. I surfaced from catatonia and started to get tense. She told me to stay still but I was getting riled. The burning incense was very hot and only a couple of millimeters away. I flinched in agitation and the glowing tip touched me. I started to shout that she had to let me go. She used the knife to cut me out and screamed at me that I should not have moved. There were two bad burns on my dick, which she said were my fault. Her daughter came back that afternoon.

After we had all lived together for about two weeks, Zooey hardly spoke to me anymore, and her daughter had had enough of whatever adult men there were in the world. Trying to ingratiate myself into their little family, I offered to help with her bath. They had a strict ritual that I didn't know about, involving a certain number of buckets of warm water poured over her head. When I tried to wash her hair with the faucet, her daughter started to cry. Zooey ran into the bathroom and called me an idiot and slapped me. Her daughter was shaking in her arms and howling that I didn't do the buckets. I was embarrassed. Zooey slept in her daughter's room that night.

The next day, I borrowed the car to visit some friends. They wanted to watch the movie *Happy Gilmore*. I was so lonely and sour about whatever my life was that, when it was over and they were all getting ready to go, I kept on suggesting other Adam Sandler movies we could watch. They could tell I was having a bad time, but after about forty-five minutes of genially enduring my almost pleading lumpy sag, they bailed.

When I drove back to the duplex, there was no one there, and no note or message about where they had gone. The microwave was also missing. I ran around the little rooms and the backyard, looking for clues while becoming more despondent and more obsessed. Cranking a Tejano record out on the patio and playing a little bell along with it, I hoped maybe the neighbors would hear me and visit. The sun was going down, so I went to a movie, trying to make the time pass and shut off my brain, hoping that when I got back, Zooey would be home. I drove around in the dark for an hour after the movie was over to nudge my wish into coming true. When I got back, the lights were black and no one was there.

She had rolled out an enormous throw rug on top of the carpet of the bedroom, but it was so big that it didn't fit. A third of it was still rolled up. On top of it was her beat-up fake Queen Anne dresser. I became unhinged and rifled through her drawers. I found a small collection of cheaply published bondage and body modification magazines put out by the very famous modern primitive originator. Zooey was featured in a three-page article, being tied up and beaten by another woman. I got on my knees and tried and tried to jerk off to the photos but was so frustrated and sad that I couldn't come. On and off throughout the night, I would pull the magazine out and try again to cum into sanity.

I fell asleep around 6 a.m. and woke up a couple hours later. I was alone the whole of the next day. Under the sink, along with some other tools, I found a hatchet. I left it on the middle of the living room carpet, thinking it was funny that, unless I moved it, it would *be* an eternity hatchet and it would *be* the awful cosmos. From somewhere else I had a couple packs of Chinese funeral joss paper and glued the sheets like a collage to decorate the nightstand and bookcase all over. It occurred to me that I was starting another semester of college in a few weeks, so I tried to clean out a little utility shed in the yard where I thought I might be able to do homework. Try as I might, it was completely under the control of the Lords of Spider and Ladies of Dirt. I was defeated; I failed and went back into the house.

Sitting in the lotus position on the couch with the TV turned down, a slow realization that all these kinds of people, all these kinds of things, were going to happen to me all the time. The thought formed as a clover made of lead. It floated

47

up from below through the heating grate, hovered next to the ceiling fan for a moment, then shot like a bullet into my chest. Blood sputtered onto my folded thighs and I spelled *Youze deserves this* in darkening cursive with my finger.

The next morning, I woke up to the sound of Zooey unlocking the door and her daughter crying. I had fallen asleep sitting there, and the TV was still on. Without saying hello, she laughed, "Are you meditating?" then told me to help her carry the microwave back in. I asked her where she'd been the last two days, and she said she was staying at a motel with her friend to eat popcorn and relax. She looked at the hatchet on the floor and the newly outfitted bookcase, then she took a half-empty pint of tequila from her purse, pulled it to fully empty, and told me this wasn't working out. I moved back in with my parents again and again and again that morning. They were not surprised then, nor were they ever.

RANDOM BEAUTY
AT SEX CLUB

In my early twenties, I was dating a woman named Doris
Anders who, when she was near me, caused an infinite,
obsessive curtain of fire to loop and obliterate my every other
thought: *I have to break up with you. I have to break up with you.
I have to break up with you.*

She was an ordeal to be with, but I was a sucker, so it took
me forever to get away. Sometimes I think we dated for a
year; sometimes I think we dated for five. I had no sense of
self. She asked me to marry her and I said yes without understanding. She was controlling, made fun of my interests, had
a cube for a head, and was rude to my family. We took a trip
to India together right after we both graduated from college
and she, whiter than white, elected daily to wear a salwar
kameez or sari.

After the trip, we lived with her mean, redneck parents.
Once, her mom, who I had talked to at least three hundred
times, pulled a revolver on me, saying she didn't know why
I was in her house. I knew how she felt.

My job then was as a "job coach" with people who had
intellectual disabilities. I was supposed to be a liaison
between the service office and the store or movie theater

or factory where they worked. But the vast majority of what I actually did for hours was observe people who had been at their place of employ for, like, fifteen years and therefore had it absolutely well in hand straightening shelves of deodorant, tearing movie tickets, or putting candles in a box. To do this kind of work is boring. The banderole motto unfurled o'er the heraldic crest of those of us tasked with merely watching someone do this kind of work was LIFE HAS NO FAVORITES.

Several months into this wonderful world, I was waiting, as usual, for as long as possible to go to this job, lying fully dressed on our bed in her parents' house and facing the wall. Doris was also about to leave for work. Something inside me finally shifted and I said, "I am breaking up with you."

"What the fuck are you talking about?"

"I have to tell you something that you are not going to understand."

"What is it, asshole?!"

"Beburba BU GUGa ging gung goo BOO goog."

"FUCK YOU YOU STUPID PIECE OF SHIT GET OUT!"

I lived in my car for about a week before I moved into my friend's laundry room.

One good thing about Doris was that she was into the idea of being bad. She told me about a sex club in San Francisco that was queer, hetero, trans, everything. Everyone did everyone there. However, one of the many bad things about Doris "being bad" was that she didn't give a fuck about my feelings or thoughts.

My dad was more or less a junkie, so I asked Doris not to tell me when she was going to smoke dope. Like a lot of people who grow up with family members who go too far with drugs, I was afraid of trying them, and it made me achingly uncomfortable even being around drugs at all. The whole issue made me feel wrung out and keenly addled. Doris didn't really care. Even though she could get high whenever she wanted and just keep quiet about it, she liked to tell me when and with whom she did it and watch my heart get beat down.

One night, a couple of months before I managed the mush-mouthed relationship prison break, she said she was going to go out and get high with a friend named Bald Aldo. I told her I was going to that sex club without her. She always tried to act like it was cool with her that we had an ostensibly open relationship, but she couldn't really deal with it. I knew her self-image as a superfreak was too important to her to ask me not to go, but I also knew it would make her nuts.

This club let trans women, MTF cross-dressers, and cis women in for some absurd discount. I cross-dressed a lot then and was broke, so I put my hair up in barrettes, wore a plaid skirt, fishnets, a bra, see-through panties, and red jelly heels. I was cuter when I was younger, so it looked good. I was a little nervous about being harassed on my way to the club's door, but I found a parking spot that was just a couple blocks away and it was fine.

I paid my negligible ladies' entrance fee and went in. For no good reason, I didn't want to bum Doris out too hard by full-on fucking anyone, so my plan was to only be a foot queen that night. I thought asking people if I could lick their boots and shoes would be an easy way to approach them, and it would not be too embarrassing if they said no. I loved being a pliable little toy then, so even refusals would be fun.

51

As soon as I walked in, I saw this hot older man wearing a shiny, black, quasi-military rubber uniform with a matching peaked cap and stilettos. I got down on my knees, put my hands around his ankles, and started to shine his shoes with my lips. He grinned a huge grin for about a minute and then shouted, "GET OFF ME, YOU FOUL FOOL!" in a hilarious croon-y croon and stormed away. One of the people who worked there saw this and we giggled about it. I felt like I belonged.

I crawled around, offering my services. Some people said yes, and some people scurried away. There was a muscle biker slowly and deeply humping a normal, tanned blond woman over a stool. They were paid by the club to be there because no one else looked anything like them. A witchy-looking drag queen was offering free shocks from an electrostimulation wand. It felt strange and good. A death-rock girl who had a humongous bust and was wearing sunglasses inside asked me to leave and go home with her in an unnervingly quiet but abrasive voice. I had a funny feeling she was going to kill me, so I declined.

There were a few Depression-era-looking ne'er-do-wells lurking in the corners, but people didn't pay them any attention. Mostly it seemed like everyone there was from the Other Side and the overall feeling was kind of sweet despite the low light, tricklings, and fleshy miscellany of background noise. A teenager who was dressed as a baby worked there at some kind of weird juice bar setup. She seemed like she was on downers. There was no booze. Creeps kept trying to touch her, but she would make donkey hee-haw noises when they did. None of them knew what to do. After talking for a bit, she and I were drawing with crayons at the juice bar. I had no idea if this was dirty, funny, or sad.

This could not have actually happened but, while coloring with the teen baby, I remember a sound like an alarm bell ringing as a troupe (there is no other way to describe it) of ten or twelve Vietnamese trans women clicked in and seemed to take over the entire palace. One was named Ivy. She was hot with a capital H. I recognized her and knew her name because my friend used to date her and he never got over it. She walked right up to me and slipped her perfect fingers into my panties and started to jack me off. I tried to put my hand up her blouse, but she kept saying, "Later is better, later is better." The little bit I copped felt like her boob was a beanbag chair.

She said, "Hey, little mommy, let's fuck," but I got nervous about breaking my own rule. I licked her feet while she politely stroked the back of my head. She waited through it for a couple of minutes but wanted cock. Ivy, a polite gummy bunny, kissed my cheek and split.

It was getting late, and my mouth felt like it had been to a lot of places it did not belong. They had mouthwash in a Sparkletts water cooler, which helped, but it still felt like it would be time to jet after I walked a final lap round the jizzcapade.

They had little cubbies where some people were paired off. In one was a God's-true-plan couple. They were both cross-dressed MTF. One was Black; the other was white. The Black person wore white lingerie and garters; the white person wore black lingerie and garters. The Black person wore a platinum wig and the white person wore a dark brown wig, and they both wore shiny mirror high heels. The room they were in was hospital-themed; they were on a gurney, making out. I asked if I could come in and lick their shoes while they were at it. They both looked at each other and started to use sign language. It was clear that they could hear me fine, but it appeared neither of them could speak. It filled my heart with a deep gratitude for what earthlings could be.

They let me kiss their shoes while they kissed and dry humped. As they folded into each other, glowing toward completion, they let me know it was time for me to go. Love floated all around them as they disappeared into the embrace.

SMOKE BOOBS

There was a little club I used to go to that had two rooms divided by a rickety door. The place was already small enough but, divided in half, you could fit maybe twenty-five people in each section. A lot of times, the door's hinges would come out of the doorframe, and the bartender would leap over the bar and pull out a mallet and a jar of putty he kept under a lounge chair in the corner and hammer them back in.

Every weekend, I was somewhere alone and, one weekend, I was alone there. I liked going back and forth between the two rooms. One was playing freestyle and early techno and the other was playing darkwave '80s. This was and still is everything I ever wanted to dance to. I wasn't super lit, but I had a couple to get loose. A woman who was about ten years older than me pushed herself way up into it. There was no hello or warning; she just materialized all the way against me. She was wearing a cool dress, had cool hair, was super curvy, and had an unusual-but-kind-of-crashed-into-looking face. She didn't really acknowledge me except for meatishly, I guess. But she didn't smell fucked-up or anything, so we kept dancing.

After about twenty minutes, as magically as she had grinded up into me, she swooshed away out from me and through the withered dividing door, waving her hands above her head. I stood there for a moment, staring and wondering. Then the bounce man tapped me on the shoulder and gave me a look that said *Dude?!* so I followed her.

As soon as I entered the other space, I saw Lily. I had had it for her for a hundred years. She was a friend of one of my coworkers named Armando that I knew from my job at the record store. A lot of my time there was spent playing a game where I tried to see if I could get through an entire day not doing any actual work. I found that if I walked around pretty fast and was carrying the cordless phone, the manager never said anything. It was almost more work than the actual job, but, then as now, I dug the insipid, childish kick of getting away with something pointless.

I first became aware of Lily when I saw that she had a sticker of a band I used to be in on her little truck. No one liked us, and I was elated by this small recognition. I jammed my hands into my pockets and kicked at the grass, smiling. While I was staring at it, I saw her come out of the apartment the truck was parked in front of. She was openly trans, short, goth, and almost unfathomably gorgeous. Basically, she was a *dreeeeeeeam.* Lily walked quickly by me and, for all the reasons one would assume, seemed creeped out that there was a creep ineptly adoring her car. She got in and drove away quickly.

Later, when she came into the record store to talk to Armando, I told him I was obsessed with her. He said, "Yeah, she's cool," then he tried to kiss me. He was a good guy, but I wasn't into him. As if by mojo hand, I started to run into Lily with increasing regularity and obtusely sort of flirted with her every time. She was always friendly, but I never got the feeling she was into me.

At the dance place that night, though, she looked straight into me, smiled real, real big, and gave me a huge, tight, long hug and skipped away. *Holy fuck,* I thought, *is it finally on?* Armando was there, and when I looked at him, he raised his eyebrows and gave the double thumbs-up.

Across the room was the woman I'd been dancing with before. She saw me and opened her mouth really wide and clacked her tongue at me. I couldn't tell if this was a countdown-to-murder gesture or an unusually aggressive countdown-to-punching-her-dance-card gesture. I just stood there and watched Lily go back through the door I'd just come through. She looked over her shoulder at me a couple times as she crossed the room. Then the woman was somehow again pushing up against me to the beats.

The night continued like this, over and over, crusted with goofer dust. The woman would suddenly whisk herself on and then off me to then vanish into the other room. Right after, Lily would come back through the door. She and I never danced, but she would talk to me and touch my arm and hug me a lot. She seemed as fainthearted and uncertain as I was, but clearly neither of us really were. The woman, who never asked for my name nor told me hers but who shall here be baptized Mysterious Vibes, would lick my neck while we were dancing but not in a sensual way—it was more like she was trying to clean off ice cream she'd wiped on me.

The little club was closing, even though it was only midnight, and everyone ballooned outside. By chance and by fate, Lily and the woman were standing next to each other, chatting with a guy I had seen around a lot. He and about four other people said they were going to hang out at some house and asked if I wanted to go. We all seemed to know each other in a way and piled into a faded red cargo van half filled with wooden fruit crates but no seats. Lily and I pretended to not-on-purpose end up in the back, behind some of the boxes.

We started to make out, and it was like six hundred million candles were burning around us. Her body was out of control and fit exactly into the shape of mine. Her mouth was like a poem. I could tell she had the same sense of surprise and delight at the enchanted taiga gluing us together. She took my hands and rubbed them all over herself and her dress. I could feel an incredible pulsing through the fabric between her legs. Then she started making really intense meowing and hissing noises and asked, "What kind of animal are *you*?" I was losing my stupid fucking mind.

The drive was short, and I asked her if she wanted to come over to my room, which we could walk to from there. She said she would "very, very much love to" but that she wanted to stay at the house for a little while because she hadn't seen the guy that drove us there in a couple years. I was beside myself.

We sat around in this gigantic, underfurnished, crumpled Victorian house in downtown and made dumb jokes. Everyone was in a pretty good mood. Mysterious Vibes was acting a little more regular but would still once in a while disappear and then reappear in another part of the room. Mostly, she was just chatting with people and laughing a lot but not in a sinister way. It was beyond my usual abilities, but somehow I was playing it cool and not being cloying or sulky about leaving. I had waited this long; I could keep waiting—and it was nice to see Lily having a good time. Finally, in a whirlpool and luscious voice, she whispered that she was ready to go.

She went around the room saying goodbye to people and then went into the bathroom for a second. Not exercising her cauldron's power of teleportation but instead this time gliding across the ceiling and then floating slowly down, Mysterious Vibes landed in my lap. She put her arms around me and played with my ear. Lily came back in the room, saw this, and was visibly crestfallen. Her shoulders fell, her face fell, her hair fell, and her dark soul of gardenia fell.

I tried to pretend nothing had changed and slid the woman off me to an awkward standing position and walked over to Lily. She said she was leaving, and I followed her out. She would not look at me or talk to me, and I wanted so much to explain what happened but was mute or stammering, so it made me sound like I was lying. She hissed at me and then turned into a cloud of all the hummingbirds on earth, and I never saw her again. (The next time I was at work, I begged Armando to give me her number to try again. He just said, "You chump-fucked it, man," and wouldn't give it to me.)

I turned to walk back inside the Victorian house and, waiting on the porch, was the woman. She took me by the thumb and said, "Where do you live?" When we got to my room, all she said was, "I was first," and then she started to kiss me. I felt blank and lost and a not-unreasonable answer to *blank* and *lost* is messing around. She was OK at it, so I felt a little better.

Mysterious Vibes took off her clothes and started to touch my ass, and I started to suck on her tits. She said, "I'm addicted to cigarettes and I had a kid about six months ago, so my breast milk might taste like smoke."

I put my hand between her legs and started to jerk her clit. After a few seconds, she yelled, "BAH!" and whammed my hand away. She started to jerk herself and came in under a minute. She was then also dressed and heading out the door in under a minute. Trying to catch up, I asked her if she wanted me to walk her home, and she said in a screwed-up cartoon voice, "If I stay anywhere near here, I am going *going* to want to pee *pee* in your bed." She elongated the word *bed* to "beeeeeeeeeeed," ending with a loud "DUH" on the D.

Still naked and questionably half-hard, I lay on my back in bed and tried to jack off. I had no idea who to think about. Lily in Moscow shooting an ICBM of jizz through the atmosphere, or the woman in Washington, DC, launching Reagan-era smoke-flavored boob milk to intercept it? All this in the galaxy-filled night above my head?

RUBBER BABY

The movie *Cyclo* made a huge impression on me, and I decided to take a trip by myself to Vietnam. It was an uncasual decision. American tourism there—and certainly tourism for me anywhere—was not as common as it is now, and I had no money. After reading a guidebook, I figured that I could stay there for a month if I came up with $2,750, including the flight. To save this money, I spent three months recording gangly teenage ska bands in the shared living room of the crappy house where I lived. How my five housemates felt about having a bunch of kids there all the time, playing bad music badly, didn't concern me. I had a goal and it required me to take over the construct we pathetically and numbly considered a home. The day before I left, I bought a rubber baby doll to put into my tourist photos. I thought carrying it around would make me seem like I was crazy so I wouldn't be hassled, and it gave me an art project to do if I got lonely.

By the time I made my way north from Saigon to Hanoi, I was so lonely that I was repeatedly going to this small movie theater that showed a different movie every night. One of the most astonishing things I've ever experienced in my entire life occurred in this theater, during a showing of *There's Something About Mary*. To American audiences, this movie's kind of corporeal humor is pretty funny, I guess, but to the people in this theater, it was as if the whack-a-do god of laughter Gelos flapped out of the ass of Genesius, patron saint of clowns, and they both rainbow-sugar-confetti-blessed all and sundry forever and ever, amen. It was madness. As there were no subtitles and it was being live-translated by a woman with a microphone, there was a delay in laughs between people who spoke English and people who were listening to the translator. When it got the part where Cameron Díaz puts the jizz in her hair for styling gel, fucking fuck. There were a few loud cackles, and then a couple seconds later after the translator caught up, the audience was standing and screaming, pulling their shirts open, playing catch with the chairs, and literally falling onto the ground howling with a heretofore unknowably outrageous freedom of mirth. It was one of the greatest human displays of feeling I have ever seen. The laugh riot went on for at least three minutes until the translator started yelling at everyone to cool it.

The rubber-baby photos started out pretty tame: the baby in a flowering tree, the baby floating in a river, the baby next to a coconut drink, the baby being held by a scooter driver. But as the trip went on, the photos started getting more invasive and far-out: the baby next to real, dead, Agent Orange birth-defect babies in jars at a war museum; the baby next to land mine victim amputees sitting on corners, asking for change; the baby next to unexploded cluster bombs on the side of the road; the baby posed on the street in front of two people in a fistfight.

The guidebook I was using said that a couple blocks from my hotel, there was a pond and garden that was a well-known gay cruising spot. This sounded interesting, so when the sun went down, I went for a walk. In less than a minute, a maybe-attractive guy in a green turtleneck moved from a shadow and tapped my shoulder to ask if I wanted to get a beer. His name was Hang, and he looked like he was in his midtwenties. He led us to a residential side street where people sold beer off their front porches. This setup is called *bia hơi*. Some people decorated with colored lights and plants, and some people just had a little sign and a keg. The beer was very light, very fresh, and very inexpensive. I bought us a couple glasses and we stood under a tree, drinking it.

We talked about the weather, and then he suggested we go to my room. I asked him if he would be into posing for a few photos, holding the baby. He said sure, as though people asked for this twenty times a day, and then I figured people probably did ask him for stuff like this twenty times a day. He told me how much money he wanted and we walked back to my hotel. He was pleasant and quiet. For the last week and a half, I had been staying in a hotel that was just for tourists, but the guy at the desk didn't say anything. Either he didn't think we were there for anything sexual or he was just tired of dealing with me.

Hang asked if he could use the shower, and in the light of the room I could see that he was living rougher than I thought. His clothes were worn-out and his hair was dirty. When he got out of the shower, he was wearing a towel and quickly put his clothes back on, but I could see that his skin was covered in little round scars from bugbites and cigarette burns. He asked if all I wanted to do was the photos, and I said yes, and he made no fuss about anything going one way or the other.

When I handed him the baby, he acted comfortable and natural with it. His first poses were like he was trying to be sexy and, unprompted, he would remove a piece of his clothes after every few shots. I asked if he could be more wooden and neutral when he was holding the baby and he did it. He held it in his lap with his back straight. There were house geckos crawling all up and down the walls. When they chirped, it sounded like a tiny training clicker trying to get your attention.

When we were done, my heart was spinning, and my head was all over the place. To try and delete myself, I paid him many times more than what he asked. He was expressionless when he looked at the money. He said he would come back tomorrow but didn't show up, and I was relieved.

A couple of years later, the band I play in used one of the nude photos of Hang for an album cover. The record label said they were happy to use the photo but that unless we covered up his dick, most stores wouldn't carry it. In a nod to the Todd Solondz film *Storytelling*, we covered Hang with an orange rectangle. There is a huge outdoor market of bootleg CDs in Hanoi, and I used to daydream that Hang saw this record there and bought it. The whole time we were taking the photos, and then again while doing the cover, I was unsure about its rightness or wrongness, but I was always sure I was going to do it.

FLORENCIA OCHOA

Right out of high school and on and off for about nine years, before I started making a living playing in bands, I taught preschool. One of the schools I worked at was open from 6 a.m. to 6 p.m., and some of the children were there for the entire twelve hours. Most of the staff were idiots. One person, though—Florencia, who was about eighteen—was emotionally developed enough to recognize that the children who were still there in the afternoon had been there all day and needed extra attention. I appreciated this about her, and we got along. She was also into music and wasn't a right-wing nutjob.

We lived close to each other, and I started to drive her home from work. I liked her as a person and she was cute, but she was way too young and not really my type at the time. While I was driving, she would put her hand between my legs and tell me she wanted us to sleep together. I would get instantly hard but just laugh and mumble that we worked together, so it wasn't a good idea. This went on for a while, and nothing else happened other than my watching her climb up the ruined steps to her studio apartment, jerking off in the car, cumming alone, and then feeling like I'd behaved responsibly.

65

I didn't have to be at work until noon, so I usually stayed up late, working on music and then watching rented movies and drinking Smirnoff Ice in bed. When I was driving Florencia home one day, she was in a horrible mood and ignored me when I asked her what was up. Around eleven that night, I heard people fake barking like puppies outside my window. I was watching *The Mummy*, eight bottles in and bloated. I looked out to see that it was Florencia and a friend of hers, Mindy, who was even younger than she was. Florencia was giving me the up-yours gesture, and Mindy was waving. This seemed bad.

Somehow, I wobbled to the door and let them in, but wobbled right back into bed. When Florencia came into my room, she looked mad. Mindy was behind her and looked nervous. Florencia walked up to me, reached into her purse, and pulled out an open bag of white baking flour. She threw it at my face but missed, and the bag thumped against the headboard without exploding. I was so drunk, I didn't react much beyond a mushy ha-ha and half-assedly flicking the half-assed bag missile back at them. She was furious and clomped out. Mindy shrugged and then left too. There were two sets of white-flour teen-angel footprints following each other out, dusted o'er the disgusting rug in my pay-by-the-week room.

The next day at work, I teased her a little about the failure of her cookie assassination plot. The other staff who worked there were so uptight that hearing she'd even come over to my house at night would have stirred up a very, very tiresome scandal, so I didn't push it. This was Friday, and she told me Mindy was having a party and that I should come. I felt that because I had made fun of her, I should go, even though a party at someone's house who I barely knew—let alone someone who was likely still in twelfth grade—sounded ghastly. I figured I would show up around midnight, drink a bunch of free booze, and ride my bike home.

I arrived at what I thought was on the late side to find that no one else had shown up yet. Only Florencia and Mindy were there; Mindy's parents were out of town. I was annoyed with the hosts and more ashamed than usual of myself. They were clearly expecting a lot of people. There were tons of food and cheapo liquor. I grabbed two six-packs and found a room filled with VHS tapes, a bunch of pillows, and a VCR. Tonite was just like any other nite.

Closing the door, I began to shotgun the beers and watch action movies to be even stupider. I could hear people start coming into the house. I was relieved the party-throwers weren't wasting so much food or dignity, but I knew I wouldn't know anyone, so I stayed where I was.

An hour and half later, Florencia burst through the door. She was wasted and I was wasted. She sat next to me, pushed her hand in my pants, and started licking my neck. She whispered, "Let's do it, come on, let's do it." As one would expect, booze was the master, and I let go. She led me into a dark bedroom.

We took our clothes off and started messing around. It was a blur of not-terrible drunk sex and kissing. She had a very wide ass and very thick legs; it was a lot of surface area. After a while, we were going at it from behind and I started to feel something uncomfortable on my cock. It was hard and granular. I kept going, but it got worse and started to hurt so much, I told her I needed to stop. Even though the lights were off, I could see there was a door to the bathroom. I got up to check it out. When I turned on the light, I saw that I was covered in shit. It was all over my stomach, chest, pubic hair, and legs. Instantly, I was sober. She had taken a shit while we were fucking. That was what was hurting my cock.

I turned the lock to the bathroom door and jumped into the shower. She started banging on it and asking me over and over what was going on and if I was OK. I just kept on scrubbing and yelled that I was fine and not to come in. She kept asking more and more tremulously and then suddenly was quiet. From under the door, I could see she had turned on the bedroom light and now knew what had happened.

As I opened the door to go back in, I understood for the first time that we were in Mindy's parents' room. They had a white bedspread and it was smeared with grubby chunks and ooze. I started cackling uncontrollably—not at Florencia but from stupefaction and hysterical panic. She started screaming at me, thinking I was laughing at her. Then she tried to stomp on me but was so drunk, she just kicked the floor really hard, twisted her ankle, and fell over. Now there was shit on the carpet too. I think I balled the bedspread up and asked her if there was a washing machine.

She screamed, "Fuck you! Fuck you! Fuck you! GET OUT! GET OUT!"

My clothes were scattered all over the room, and I tried to get dressed as quickly as I could. Florencia kept quietly repeating through gritted teeth, "GET OUT! FUCKER!" I could hear some concerned kids gathering by the bedroom door. The devil whispered to me, *Climb out the window. Climb out the window*, so I did. By some miracle, my bicycle was right beneath it. I rode home and away, down overly empty streets and overly empty hills in the inappropriate moonlight, feeling inappropriately free.

After a few years, we became friends again and will absolutely never talk about this. A week ago, she told me she was getting married and invited me. If I don't go to the wedding without a date, looking good but not great, and don't bring a real, real, real nice present, God will strike my entire family dead.

DALE BIANCHI

I was in a bunch of other bands before the one I am in now. When I first started getting more serious about music, I didn't know how anything worked, but I felt I should be willing to do anything to *make* it work. Dale told me he was in the major-label music business and could help me out. He mailed me his business card, a CD-R of a Nine Inch Nails covers album with some legitimately big artists on it, and a bunch of records by a group called Pale Diary that sounded like they might play arenas in Europe but were totally unknown in the United States. He had giant, frosted, Hollywood-style salon hair. This all seemed too good to be true. I was ready to be famous.

We talked on the phone about the right people he knew, and he told me how to make a press kit for our demo. I spent days and days making them, put them into big, expensive, metallic-green envelopes, and mailed them to him express. He told me he passed them on to all his label contacts, and then he asked me if I wanted to meet and go out. Of course I said yes, no distress.

When Dale arrived at my place, I whooshed him immediately out the door to hide the truth of the garbage dump and the five to eight other garbage men and boys who were living there with me. We planned to walk to the little strip of bars and dance clubs downtown and decided we would get a drink in each one.

It took about twenty minutes to get there, and I had a plan to impress him on the way. There was a billboard advertising a bank over a little bridge we had to cross. The band I was playing in had adopted as its emblem a valentine's heart with the number thirteen in it. I had this as a tattoo from before I'd started playing, and the band had decided to use it. In the ad on the billboard we would pass was a similarly shaped heart.

I said, "Hey, give me a minute."

I pulled out a can of black spray paint I had planted in some bushes and climbed on the railing of the bridge and then onto the billboard. I sprayed a 13 in the middle of this heart. Victory!

"Oh, uh . . . wow. Do you do that a lot?"

Outside of the fourth or fifth spot we went to, I ran into Michelle Phommathep. She was out with her sisters and cousins, celebrating her birthday. She said she had turned eighteen that night. When she was fifteen, she sent me a love letter on light-pink-glitter construction paper with her phone number. At the bottom of it she'd written, *Remember age ain't nothing but a number.* Even at fifteen, she looked stupendously fuckable, but I was a Christian, so all I did was jerk off to her for three years after calling her to thank her for the sparkly note.

She walked right up to me and exhaled in my ear, "Am I grown up enough now?" I felt like I was going to cum in my pants. She laughed while walking away with her party and told me to call her.

Dale and I went into the next place, called The Usual. It was mobbed, and we crushed onto the dance floor. He handed me a gin and handed a cute guy next to me a gin. The cute guy never stopped looking at the floor. A minute later, the three of us were grinding and dancing; I was in the middle, Dale in the front, and Cute Guy behind. This was not what I expected from our business meeting, but I was determined. As tightly jammed as I was against Dale's ass, he managed to reach behind himself and squeeze his palm against my balls. I, in turn, reached back into Cute Guy's pants and started to rub his dick. We were all squishing each other in time to the song, but after a minute, Cute Guy ran away. I was not attracted to Dale and, with the trio spell now broken, told him it was too stuffy and that I wanted to go outside.

We got overrated limoncellos at a mobster's defrocked limoncello place and then went next door to a coffeehouse that served what felt to me like classy bottled beers. I liked this place because you could drink, and it was also bright enough that you could read. Since it was ostensibly a coffee place, you didn't look as untethered or hope-free as you might when reading in a bar.

Some kid I didn't know walked up to us and said he dug my band, and then he and his friends started chanting "Caterpillar! Caterpillar! Caterpillar!" This was a break-dance move, sometimes called "the Worm," that they knew that I liked to do for some reason. The stars were aligned so perfectly. Dale could see strangers were into my miserable band, and I could show off again.

You can start the Caterpillar lying down flat, but to really commit to its deserved majesty, you leap forward in a high arc and catch yourself by the hands and chest on the ground with your legs curled up over your back. All or nothing, I jumped up and out, and my chin smashed hard into the polished concrete floor. I was wearing a white T-shirt and when I stood up, blood spurted all over it. The whole room went, "OOOOOOOOOH!" I still have a scar from this.

Dale and I split.

We staggered about two blocks and he pushed me against a streetlamp. He pulled down my pants and started sucking my cock. The blood was still pouring down from my chin; it was getting all over his face and in his hair. Blood was mixing with spit and pre-cream. This was a weekend and a crowded area; lots of people were walking by, watching the blood and sucking, so we stopped and went on staggering back to my place.

When we got there, he started blowing me again. The telephone rang and it was Michelle. She and I immediately started having phone sex. This ring-a-ding three-way got me super excited, and I came really fast and big. It caught Dale off guard and he kind of shouted, "ARGH!"

Michelle heard him and screamed, "Is there someone else there with you?!" and hung up.

Michelle now runs an unimaginably prosperous cosmetics brand. We hung out a little, a couple years ago. She's even hotter as a grown-up and because of that and because of her success, she's also, in an appealing way, supremely intimidating. We never messed around after we reconnected, although we did have phone sex again twice, reliving past ardors.

Dale was so drunk, he didn't realize I was on the phone the whole time, and he sat bolt upright. The moon was full and shone through the window directly on him. There was red-black blood drying and mixing with my sheen of just-sucked-out-and-pulled jack; it was a rose in glimmering candlelight all over his face and hair. Little clots had formed and woven themselves into his mountainous bleached tips. He lurched out the door, and I don't know how he got home.

A few months later, still a believer, I visited Dale at his place in Los Angeles. His apartment was a little one-window studio with a Murphy bed. This wasn't the first time someone in the music business had lied to me and certainly wasn't the last. All twelve of the press kits I'd sent him were in the corner in a box. Even though his place was small, I wondered why he at least didn't hide them.

1 - (8 1 8) - K I M M I E - M O O R E

I used to work as a dishwasher in delis and bakeries as a teenager. It was rotten in the flattest way possible. My hands were cracked and the palms bled all the time. I stole thick black rubber gloves from the chemistry lab of my high school to try and keep them dry, but it didn't work.

An extremely irritating kid in my eleventh-grade English class, Jeffrey Yam, made a hot dog announcement that he was applying for a summer job at Brentano's Books at the Northridge Mall. It was a chain that faked being wood-paneled and fancy. I hated this kid, and I hated my last two years of washing dishes. During his proclamation, he waved around his application and I asked if I could see it.

His only prior work experience was volunteering at his church two years before, but he wrote a long personal statement about loving Flaubert. He would pull shit like interrupting class to tell everyone how stupid he thought my clothes and hair were and that I was a huge faggot. He also loudly claimed to be the smartest and most "culturally refined" person in the entire school. I knew I had to get the job instead of him, not only to fuck him over but also to rescue my destroyed hands.

There was no way I could get hired with my references

being East Side Bagels, Taco Bell, and Choco Churro, so I wrote down some phony jobs—I said I had taught karate for three years at an after-school program where my mom worked, knowing she would lie for me if they called. But what I hoped would really send me over the top was using the phone number for the Style Council fan club in London. I found it on a card inside a record and wrote it down as the contact of a made-up relative's sheet-music store where I said I worked while I was a made-up exchange student. I assumed they wouldn't make a long-distance call to England to check it and that they would be impressed.

After a brief interview with the delightfully swishy manager, who was obvious about liking that I was wearing a yellow paisley tie and pink socks, I got the job. Fuck You Jeffrey Yam, Fuck You. He was flabbergasted, infuriated, and ashamed, and he stopped messing with me for the remaining couple months before summer. Although the job also proved to be catatonically boring, my hands eventually healed and, along with every other employee, I stole wagonloads of books. As a consequence, I read a lot. While still working there a year later during the summer after I finished high school, a woman walked in and asked for a job application. She was attractive, wore flattering glasses, and seemed to want to talk to me. I was behind the cash register and I had to stand there anyway, so we chatted for a bit. When she returned with her filled-in application, I made a show of looking it over like I was cool and had something to do with hiring people. We talked for at least an hour. Her name was Kimmie Moore and, according to her application, had just graduated from La Sierra University. She was twenty-two.

I was eighteen and did not realize she was flirting with me super hard.

Jeffrey had come in and reapplied about three months after I started and, sadly for him, handed his application to me. I put greasy fingerprints all over it and jammed it to the bottom of the stack where, after placing Kimmie's at the top of the stack, I checked to make sure his remained stillborn where I had left it ten months before.

Kimmie started to call the store a lot, and we talked on the phone while I rang people up. She was smart and pretty funny, which made the time go fast. She never asked for my home number, nor I hers. After a couple weeks, she invited me over for a party. In an attempt to seem bookish (job and all), I told her I didn't like parties, but really, I was just shy. She was persistent and called a couple more times with the same invite, saying how amazing it would be. On the day of this now-folkloric party, she called again, and I finally got the address and said I would come after work. It wasn't that far from the mall.

I knocked on the door and saw that there was no party there at all. There was only Kimmie's three housemates sitting around a dining room table playing cards, wearing swim trunks, and drinking beer. It was like a three-panel comic strip of disaffection. They started laughing at me when I walked in and teasingly asked me when I'd graduated high school. I was flustered and disoriented. I made up a story about being hit by a car and missing a year of school so that even though I just got out, I was nineteen. They laughed some more, too loudly, but thankfully let it go. Kimmie looked at the ceiling, said nothing about a party, and led me to her bedroom.

Her spot was small and girly, lilac and rose, a little messy but not dirty. We sat on her bed and, as was easy between us, talked for several hours. Her very big dog walked in and out, pushing the door open to leave or enter with its long snout.

We got wrapped up in talking, and it became late. I still lived with my parents, and it was past 1 a.m. They were OK if I stayed out until whenever, but I had to call them to say when I would be home. I wasn't going to do this in front of Kimmie, so I said I needed to leave to go to work early the next day, which was also true. She told me in a kitten's voice that I should stay, and she started to kiss me. I was still a virgin, so I only thought as far as *Fuck it! All right! Making out!* After some fair-haired and pleasant just-kissing, I told her I needed to get up and use the bathroom.

I stood before the toilet with a valiantly youthful erection. When one has such an erection, the body makes it physiologically difficult to pee to avoid mixing the sacred with the profane. I stood there and stood there, waiting for the piss to come out. I was becoming worried that she would think I was taking a dump for, like, fifteen minutes.

As I was walking back, I was trying to come up with a joke to clear away her presumed revulsion, but when I opened the door, Kimmie was now wearing only a short white T-shirt: no pants, no socks, no blouse, and no panties. Like a giant's bell, a voice in my head rang out, *Tonight, you will do it.* I think that, because of my being abused and her having really poor boundaries, my mom also entered into and sat upon my mind, despite the fact that there was a very cute, cool-seeming, very-ready-to-get down, half-naked woman waiting in front of me. This was a problem for years and years. It wasn't that

I pictured my mom in any sexual capacity. It was that she would materialize to rate my performance, or hover over the bed while I tried to fuck whoever I was with in a way this mom ghost would approve of, or just be very present, mopping the floor and muttering about how pissed she was that I had come home from school to disturb her. Kimmie turned out the lights.

We started to kiss some more, and she took my clothes off. In addition to this being my debut, I had never been fully naked with anyone before. She looked good and had big breasts. They were workable and soft; I tried to lick beneath her nipple in a way a friend's older rockabilly sister had told me to do. This sister also told me that to be good in bed, you had to go down on a woman. I had never done that either.

To my absolute horror, her vagina was incredibly cruddy and could not have smelled more against the law. I thought, *Jesus, how am I going to do this for the rest of my fucking life.* I started to audibly gag and choke but knew I had to keep trying. After a minute of me hacking up in her hole, she pulled me off of her. At one point, for some reason, my mom thought it was appropriate to tell me that giving a woman head was an acquired taste, so I thought I would be prepared, but I was stunned. *Go away, Mom!* I thought for the first time in what would be years and years of thinking *Go away!* while fucking.

After I ate out a woman the second time, I realized Kimmie must have had some kind of unfortunate cake infection, and I was incredibly relieved, for my future as envoy to the ways of my friend's older rockabilly sister, that this condition was not the common state of vaginal sovereignty. Only years later did I think of how mortified she might have been to have had such an ill-equipped dork teenager garroted by her slit's murk.

She didn't give any indication of how she felt about my dramatic-but-not-disproportionate reaction, though, and moved down to put my cock into her mouth. Perhaps she wanted to avoid my eyes but, with no effort, she sucked it all the way to the base. Oddly, she just sort of left it there without moving or licking, just resting it all the way inside her mouth. It did feel very nice in a sleeping-bag kind of way, and after she came back up a couple minutes later, trying to talk dirty, I told her how "freakin' all right" it felt. In a long night of firsts, this was also my first real blow job.

It was still AIDS-will-kill-you days, so she handed me a condom. I had been buying or stealing them and my mom had been leaving boxes of them on my dresser since I was fifteen. I'd practiced putting them on and would jerk off into them, so I was ready. I tore the packet open and composedly rolled it down.

Another thing I'd learned from my friend's sister was that there are a lot of positions and that variety is the spice of life. I also thought this might be the only time I might ever fuck, so I figured I better jam through them all. I put my cock inside of her and began with artless, lagomorphic Cro-Magnetism to descend. After a few seconds, I would steer her into one pose, pump a few times, then steer her into another pose and shove a few more times. She was thick in a good way—thicker than would have allowed me to just toss her around—so her attending to the gymnasium of my love had to have required some tolerant agreeability on her part. The descriptions and rough drawings by the rockabilly sister ticked away.

When I got through the list, I would start again. No one stance seemed to feel any better or worse than the others; in fact, I didn't feel much sensation at all. Condom, nerves, the flood of matriarchal images, and not settling into any position's groove for very long led to my taking forever to cum. Kimmie just kind of allowed me to knead and roll her up. Once in a while, I would stop concentrating on what I learned from the book and she would meet my eyes with a probably baffled Juliet's gaze.

After a week and a half, I finally came and felt just glad to have it done with. I, as instructed by the pamphlet, carefully withdrew myself from her and gripped the bag so as to not allow a leak. Then, as not instructed by the pamphlet, I threw it on the rug.

She wrapped her big, curvy body around me and held tight. The last bit of advice from the sister and my mother was that women wanted to be held after sex. I told myself that I would stay for twenty minutes and after that had to go. I fixed onto the digital clock, wanting so much to leave.

Kimmie kissed me a little more, and I kissed her a little more, and then, feeling like I needed to make an excuse for everything, said, "I've never done this before." She paused the kissing, perhaps taking in that I had been a virgin and perhaps then adding up my unnatural techniques and maybe making more sense of them. Looking away, she said out of the side of her mouth, "I've never done this before either." For a second, I thought she might have been confiding her virginity to me, too, but then I understood that she was making a joke about how strangely I'd fucked her.

The twenty minutes passed and on the dot I told her that I had to leave. I tried to stand up but she held me very firmly and physically would not let me go. At first it seemed like a game, but the more I struggled, the more tightly she coiled around me. After using all my strength, I was able to burst from her grasp and tried to laugh, but she just stared at me, very much not laughing. Her dog pushed the door open. walked right over to the condom on the rug, sniffed, and then ate it.

When I got to work the next morning, I was exhausted, discombobulated, and involuntarily exhilarated. I lay down on a block of newspapers in the back room. One of my coworkers, Shlomo, who was later fired for sexual harassment, started asking me why I was so worn-out. Then he started doing a little dance and singing a little song about how I'd gotten laid the night before and was too boned-out to work. I felt some pride that this was finally the case.

I knew I needed to call the next day, which I did. Kimmie said I should come over, and I did. When I got to her house, she told me her housemates were being rowdy and that we could just talk by my car. She asked if she could see my driver's license photo. I don't know if she really just wanted to see an ugly photo or if she wanted proof of my age. I figured I should tell her I lied and that I was really eighteen, dimly hoping she might think it was adorable. She did not. She made an exasperated squeak, reared back, and punched me in the stomach so hard, I fell onto the ground. Still, there's always something about the person you lose it to.

She started calling my house after that, even though I never gave her my home number. She started to call a lot.

I would always talk to her, even after I started dating someone else. One night, she suggested we meet up on Ventura Boulevard and go for a drive. I thought it was weird that she didn't ask to meet at her house, but then I was glad she didn't ask to come to mine.

When I saw her, she was wearing a huge, 1980s, Patti LaBelle-style hairdo and a very tight, very chic mauve dress. Her car was enormous; I didn't remember seeing it before. I got in and we drove all around the outskirts of the Valley. We mostly weren't talking and had the radio on. After about an hour, we stopped by her friends' house. She hadn't told me we were going to go there. I don't think she told them to expect us, either, because they seemed super perplexed when she showed up and also super annoyed that she'd brought over someone they didn't know.

Her friends were two acne-plagued, rapier-wit, substantially hostile nerds. They shared a small BO-scented room and had covered the walls with Michael Jackson posters. There were a couple of framed letters that were from Michael Jackson too. They also had maybe three hundred thousand comics on the floor between their beds, on the shelves, and on the beds. They had a coffee table in the middle of the room with matching electric typewriters facing opposite each other. We'd apparently interrupted their writing of an anime script they said Michael Jackson himself was going to produce. Trying to be friendly, I asked a couple of questions about their relationship with Michael Jackson. They seemed sincerely disgusted and sputtered that there was no way I would ever understand. My memory of them is their faces melting.

We got back into the car and stopped a little while later in front of a park. Kimmie started to kiss me and I kissed her back. It didn't occur to me that this was foolish because I now had a normal girlfriend who I was afraid to tell her about, and that it was also foolish because she'd punched me before. It was all happening in a cloud of not-happening.

She said she hated me, laughed, and then started to drive back to where I'd left my car. It was on a busy street and there was nowhere to stop, so we parked her car a couple blocks away and then started to walk over to mine. By complete chance, two of my own friends were coming down the block toward us. I introduced everyone, and they seemed impressed by Kimmie's style and how pretty she was. I'd somehow missed it before, but her fantastically giant dog was chained to a streetlight near where I'd parked. My friends liked her dog too.

Kimmie freed The Condom Eater's beast and asked me to walk with her back to the parking lot behind some stores where we'd left her car, even though she'd just walked me to mine. I told my friends I would meet them later, and Kimmie gave them a wink. When we got to her car, she said she was going out of town and asked me to watch her dog while she was away. Standing against a wall in front of her car, she tried to give me the rhinestone leash to take him away with me that very night. I told her categorically there was no way I would or even could take care of her dog. My parents would lose their minds, and also, I did not and do not like dogs, and her dog was—as noted—a lot of dog to not like. Kimmie became furious.

She shoved her dog into her car, started it up, and inched it toward me, trying not to smash it into me but rather trying to pin me against the wall, it seemed. I could not believe what was happening, so I didn't react. Kimmie started to flip me off and honk her horn, which snapped me out of my trance, and I took this opportunity to step out of the way. She kept pulling up until her bumper tapped the wall. She continued pressing the accelerator, slowly pushing up against the building, smoke fluming from her radiator. She was still honking and flipping me off until she finished with whatever this atrocity exhibition was supposed to be, put the car in reverse, and drove away. I met up with my friends and, in a muddled way, told them what had happened. They laughed their asses off, which made it seem kind of funny to me too.

Around this time, I started to move a lot. I was bouncing between renting a garden shed and moping back to stay at whatever short-term house my mom had sorted out for her and my younger brother. By this time, my sister had a job and her own place. Although I never left a forwarding number and told my family not to give my new numbers to anyone, Kimmie always found out where I was and began to call. This went on for about two years.

During a longer stint in the garden shed, she called to invite me to a concert she'd won tickets to. About a week later, two CDs by these bands showed up at my address— an address I'd never given her. She then took to mailing me prolix letters about trips she took up the coast, breaking into people's houses and cars or sleeping in the woods. The spellbound part of me found this goth idyll both alluring and troubling. I jerked off and came on the pages.

I had a new girlfriend, and we fucked a lot in my little shack. This was back when answering machines would play your messages out loud to you while they were being left. Kimmie called at least twenty-five times and left at least twenty-five messages while my girlfriend and I were in the middle of doing it. The first couple times, I thought it was just a coincidence, but then I began to assume it would happen. The messages were pretty neutral—*Aloha, how are you?* But my girlfriend stopped coming over because she didn't want to get murdered.

By now, I was teaching preschool at some stupid, overly theoretical rich-kid school where the whitest parents in the Valley would hang out all day. Who knows why, but in a broken-down way, I gave a condensed version of this saga to a parent I didn't even really know that well. He told me it was insane and that I should call the police. I'd never felt worried about Kimmie's ways, but to mollify this father, I acted like I was now very concerned.

The garden shed where I was failingly trying to grow up and failingly trying to hide from Kimmie was infested with rats. I tried to scare them away by playing long, loud notes on my bass guitar, but it didn't work. Wayne, the guy who owned it, was a heavy-metal trust-fund kid who never stopped dressing like he was a kid, although he was probably forty. He sold heroin to and played poker with a lot of famous jazz-fusion, rock-legend, and LA bubblegum-metal drummers. Digging deep, he called this "the Drum Club." I remember them debating about whether to let Marky Ramone into the club but deciding to "pass" in the end, even though they thought his being able to play high-hat sixteenth notes with one hand was notable.

The Drum Club guys were always inexplicably nice to me and I got to jam with them in the high-end rehearsal studio

Wayne owned. I played with the drummers from Jethro Tull, Lou Reed, The Knack, David Lee Roth, Jean-Luc Ponty, and Janet Jackson. Wayne and I had a little band too. It was called . . . TECHNO PRIMAL!!!

Sometimes Wayne was really generous and sweet, but sometimes he was an unpredictably catastrophic dick and a racist piece of shit. He would take me to dinner once in a while but then do things like describe a Persian friend of mine in truly reprehensible terms to her face. He was beyond the beyond even for the '90s, but I was like a deer in his moronic headlights and didn't do anything.

Wayne was always sort of doing home improvement projects and one day told me he was going to tear down the shed. I asked when, and he said he would tear it down when he tore it down. He frequently said jive crap like this so I didn't take it too seriously.

About four months later, I was inside on the phone with my dad. He had just gotten back together with my mom, and she'd moved in with him in the Bay Area. Then I heard this incredible banging on the wall. I opened the door, and there were two workmen with sledgehammers smashing the shed down. They jumped back and started yelling. They'd had no idea I was in there. I found Wayne and asked him what the fuck. He said, "I told you I was going to do this."

My sister had a couch and I had a station wagon, so I quickly got all my stuff together and asked if I could stay with her. She wasn't happy about it because I was always an inconsiderate, controlling jerk to her, but she said yes. On my way out, I feebly and senselessly smashed the shed's windows with a wooden samurai sword (why?) that my favorite teacher had given me. I still have it and keep it by my front door to appear invincible.

It didn't work at my sister's place, and it was all my fault. I fucked my girlfriend there and wouldn't let my sister into her own apartment while we were at it. I accidentally locked myself out and I kicked the door in, breaking the doorframe. The landlord, who my sister also babysat for, was stunned into silence when he saw what I did to his guesthouse. I probably lasted about ten days there and then, at the rational insistence of my sister, asked my parents if I could move back in with them. I paid her boyfriend one hundred dollars to drive me and my stuff up from LA to Palo Alto in his van. I sold my car to Paul Roessler from the Screamers for seventy-five dollars. I later learned my sister's boyfriend had been beating her up and trying to force her into sex work.

Kimmie never called me or wrote to me at my parents' new house. I wonder how much time, if any, she spent trying to find me before quitting.

1-(408)-KIMMIE MOORE

Five characterless years passed, and I was living in San Jose, teaching preschool and trying to do music. The band I played in had a website that was set up like a Choose Your Own Adventure book. It also had photos of the people in the band and a phone number to call for booking shows. This was my home number, and I was living with another person in the band. His girlfriend took a message for me saying that "a Kimmie Moore" had called, was living in San Francisco, and that she'd left a number.

What felt like a lot of time had passed, and maybe enough things had happened in between that she had become normal. I called, and it was easy to talk to her like before, and it sounded like her life had stabilized. She worked at a book publisher and had a son.

At the school where I was working, two hours of the day were spent watching the children during nap time. It usually took about thirty minutes to get them all sorted out, and then I had an hour and half to read or do lesson plans or whatever. Every couple of days for the next week and half, I called Kimmie during nap time and we chatted and caught up—quietly, because I was in a room with twenty-one sleeping four-year-olds. It was light and amiable. Life can change. We made plans to get dinner on a Saturday evening.

This was before I toured a lot, so the hour's distance to San Francisco felt insurmountably far. I suggested we eat in Mountain View, which is roughly between where we both lived. She agreed and we set up to meet at an Indian restaurant on Castro Street.

We both arrived on time. I looked more or less the same as I did five years before—a little older, of course, but I hadn't tubbed out or gone bald. I didn't dress up but I tried to look nice. She'd put on some weight that worked with her body type but hadn't really combed her hair and was wearing a dirty sweatshirt, old dirty shorts, and outdoor gardening sandals. Before saying hello, she said in an angry voice that it was much farther for her to get there than it was for me. I tried to laugh and said that the restaurant was good.

During dinner, she said several times that I looked nice and that she looked awful. I said as many times that she looked amazing. The conversation was OK enough when it wasn't incredibly awkward, and we ate fast. I worried it might seem too gruff after the stilted torpedo of dinner to just call it a night, so I suggested we get a drink at a bar across the street. Her eyes lit up—lit up too much—and I felt very ready to go home.

During this quick half-a-beer, she began to sit closer and closer to me; it didn't really register until our thighs were touching. I was worried that if I moved away, she would capsize into telling me how awful she looked again. Since I really can't drive after even a little booze, I told her I had to split, and we walked back to our cars.

She drove a rambling, far-from-new dark blue Volvo and showed me where someone had keyed YUPPIE SCUM into the paint. We both rolled our eyes at crust punks who didn't pay attention. She hugged me goodbye and went for a kiss. I kissed her back—it was a reflex—but then immediately did not want to kiss her and really, really did not want to lead her on, especially if she had a child at home. She seemed rumpled and offended that I stopped. She didn't say anything but gave me a long, dirty look, got into her car, and sped away. I sat on a cement parking stop for a few minutes, feeling a lot of feelings. Feelings of realization; feelings of regret; feelings of compassion; feelings of broad, unpleasant wonder; and feelings of fear.

A week later, she called me at work—a number I never gave her—and demanded to know why I hadn't gotten ahold of her. Frankly, it hadn't crossed my mind, and I tried to explain that while at first I was calling her a lot to catch up, that behavior wasn't normal for me; I didn't even talk to my oldest and best friends that often. She calmed down and said I had to drive up to her place on the Fourth of July and spend it with her and her son. The Fourth of July was in two days. I had a tradition of going to a big Cineplex on the Fourth of July with two bottles of Chianti in a backpack, buying one ticket, and then sneaking into all the theaters to watch summer-bummer movies all day and get lit. I tried to explain this to her and that it was a thing for me without trying to sound too much like I didn't want to spend the day with her and her kid, which I of course did not. She was insistent and upset and berated me as "hard-hearted." To get off the phone, I said I would come up.

The next day, my cousin, who had just moved into his first non-slumlord apartment, told me he was having a Fourth of July party and invited me. He and I were really close, so I told him I would be there. As soon as I got off the phone with him, an absurdly tight, hot guy named Arturo, who I messed around with infrequently, called and said that he had become obsessed with giving people head while they were driving. He asked what I was doing the next day. I was driving my grandma's 1970s four-door Chevrolet with wide, seafoam-velour bench seats then. I told him that what I was doing the next day was just what he had asked me to do. I now had three good reasons to bail on Kimmie and one good excuse.

I was very nervous to call her but took the multiple alternate offerings as signs from God to cancel. I told her about my cousin and how important it was that I be there. It was dead silent on her side of the line for a long time. I weakly said it would be great to make plans later. It was still quiet, but I could hear her breathing. The sky turned to dust and one thousand and one crows began pecking on the window. I told her I was going to go, and as I was setting down the receiver, she screamed so loudly of death that even though the phone was an arm's length away from my ear, I could clearly hear its horrible potential.

The next day, Arturo and I completed the delectable and lively deed. Afterward, he said he had another blow-job date but wanted to go to the party later. I gave him the address and dropped him off with a gold-star thumbs-up for slut's fealty and slut's focus. When I got to my cousin's, it was a nice day. He was in a great mood and being a great host. He and about twelve of his friends were there. Someone had brought a video projector, so we hooked his PlayStation up to it and started a tournament playing the best robot-fighting game of all time: *Armored Core*. A friend of his, who was way too hot for me but that I had a long-standing crush on, smiled at me. I knew nothing would ever happen, but it was cool to get a smile. I felt really happy to be where I was.

A while before this, I had gone on a couple of dates with a woman named Diep, who had flat-out picked me up at a dance club horribly called The Edge. She was almost absurdly beautiful, had freckles and long hair, was fit, wore black clothes, and had a faraway look in her eyes. The first question she asked me when we met was if I had graduated from college, which I thought was funny. Even though she was so yummy and very nice, we didn't really click in a deep way. After she was out of town for a work thing, we didn't get back in touch when she got home. It was fine.

She and I never really fucked but the naked messing around we did was really hot for both of us. I think because of this, we didn't forget about one another, and we would leave each other oblique messages once every three or four months. A couple days after the scream from Kimmie, Diep and I met for lunch. We talked a lot and I told her the long, reminted tale of Kimmie. She too said she thought this was insane and asked me if I felt I was in trouble. I said no.

It was the first time we had seen each other in a year. We had a good time at lunch and naturally skirted around maybe hooking up again. When we were done at the restaurant, we started to kiss. She had a peculiar habit of putting about a half a second between every other word she spoke. She said, "I really . . . want to . . . fuck you . . . up the . . . ass with . . . a dildo."

93

It was really hard for me not to impersonate her cadence when I answered, but I didn't want to mess this up, so I said, evenly and without pause, "Yes, come over right now. I would love for you to do that."

We drove to my Oscar-the-Grouch house and got to it. She looked as hot as ever. I did have a couple of dildos, but I didn't have a strap-on harness. I had to use a rope to tie one of them—she picked the bigger one—around her upper thigh. It took a couple tries to get it right, but we were both getting more and more turned on, so we made it work. I put on a PJ Harvey record to try and mask our unhealthy doings from my many housemates. Diep started getting incredibly cranked up and was being deliciously loud as she pounded away.

My bedroom door had glass panes in it that I had papered over with photocopies of pictures of my music idols. There was one with Little Richard that had a caption beneath: JUST A LONELY GUY. Someone started knocking on it. With a rubber dick up my ass, I shouted, "Go away!" thinking it was a housemate being obnoxious. The knocking got harder, like it was being done with a whole fist. Diep and I looked at each other, and I yelled, "Go the fuck away NOW!" Then the knocking became hard banging, and the door's panes were rattling. Diep pulled out of me and looked freaked out.

Kimmie's voice came from behind the door. "I know what you're doing in there!"

"Jesus fuck! Fuck you! If you know what we're doing, why are you here? How did you get into my house? Leave now or I'm calling the police!"

I heard the front door slam. No one ever left any of the doors unlocked. I have no idea how she got in.

Diep said, "Was that . . . who I think . . . it was? I am . . . going to . . . go home."

Over and over, I said how sorry I was. We got dressed and, in a daze, I walked her to her car. I saw that Kimmie's Volvo was parked outside too. She wasn't in it, but this scared the shit out of me. Diep drove away, and I ran back inside and called the cops. I explained to them what had happened and that her car was still outside but I didn't know where she was. The fuzzy sounds of the dispatcher agreed that this was indeed a problem. *Finally.* I was incredibly shaken up. A housemate of mine, who was an unrepentant drag and twit, came home right as I got off the phone with 911, but when I explained what happened, he was unusually human and supportive. To be safe, he wanted to know which car was Kimmie's, and we went outside together so I could point it out to him.

She was sitting in the front seat now with her head in her hands, shaking and crying, and we could see that her son was in a car seat in the back. I felt a wave of maybe-laughable empathy and told my housemate that this was her and I felt like I should say something. I wanted to stop all this and thought if her son was there, she wouldn't do anything to me. My housemate said he would be right inside if I needed help. I knocked on her window. She winced a little when she saw me and, as she rolled down the window, I heard she was playing the same (muthafucking!) PJ Harvey record I had on while Diep and I were banging.

I told her this whole protracted, invasive, unreasonable thing had to end and that nothing like this could ever happen again. She was really sobbing now and apologizing over and over and asked if we could talk. I asked her whether talking

95

would mean she'd cool it, and she said yes. We sat on the curb and she took a few minutes to collect herself. The cops drove up and asked if things were OK. She started to cry again, and I said I felt like we could sort it out. They shrugged and drove away. My housemate poked his head out to ask the same question when he saw the cops leave.

A kid on a bike rode by and farted. It made me laugh but she didn't. She borderline raved for about forty-five minutes, trying to explain why she had behaved like this, now and before. It was hard to follow where she was trying to get to, but it seemed to be smoothing her out. Her son was still in the car. He was asleep or dead.

When it seemed like she had removed everything from inside her, she took a purposely humorous deep breath and we stood and went to her car. I said hello to her child, who was the same age as the kids in my class and was just waking up. He waved drowsily and yawned. Kimmie looked at me and said she had a question.

"I just got braces, and I want to see what it's like to kiss someone with them on?"

She put her arms around me and tried this kiss. Like a trapped pig, I grunted and scooted away. With the nonthinking, blank-eyed density of a pig at a trough, she grabbed a handful of my hair with one hand to pull me back toward her and, with her other hand, reared back to punch me in the stomach really hard. Again. A circle made of pig offal spun around over our heads like a coming storm soon to rain down acid and pig shit. I ran inside, and I don't know how or when she left. I lay on my bed, the rope and dildo still sitting on the sheets, and tried to rest my blown-apart head.

Diep called me the next day and asked how things turned out. I had a bad feeling I would never see her again, and I did not. A few days after this, Kimmie started to call too. At first, I would hang up as soon as I heard her voice, and then I would pick up and not say anything and wait for her to hang up. Once, she asked the silence if she was now banned forever. I said, "What do you think?" and hung up. Then I got a phone with caller ID, stopped picking up at all, and her calls dissolved.

About a year later, I started playing in another band that was getting a little press. Kimmie started to come to these shows. I would see her in the back, and she would stay as we were loading out. I pretended she wasn't there, and she never said anything to me. This happened three or four times.

Later that same year, I moved to Oakland and told my former housemates in San Jose not to give my new number out. When my dad died, she emailed me to say she was sorry. I wrote back with just a *Thank you.* She wrote back again and I, my nerves so frayed from grief it was important that I hold onto my life as tightly as I could, told her politely that it would be best if we remained out of contact. To my surprise, she neither called nor wrote again.

Six years later, after moving to Seattle and then back to Oakland, I was walking at night in San Francisco with a bunch of my friend's friends on our way to drink. As we approached a busy intersection, I saw Kimmie standing there by the traffic light. She saw me, too, and was cringing and raising her shoulders to look smaller. In a panic, she looked to the left and right for an escape route, holding up her hands to steel against any coming institutional retribution.

"I'm not following you! I'm not following you! I live here! This is my block!"

"Everything is OK," I said and crossed the street, not wanting to explain this to anyone.

PASTOR GUCCI

I loved teaching at the school where Florencia and I worked and tried to do a good job. Before music mania started working out OK, the overtly named Bay Area Christian School was the place I'd held a job the longest. It was part of a church and elementary school. If I was feeling loopy from too many full-on children, I would answer the phone in a NES 8-bit-inspired voice and in that voice, the directness of this school's name became super funny.

I started there just before the right wing entirely co-opted evangelicals as a manipulative and manipulable voting block. As that seeping encroachment fattened, it became an entirely oppressive and dark place to work. They made all the staff do an interview with a fascist Christian marketing group to see who did or didn't fit into their plans to become a for-profit pro-war, guns, truck, and flag charter school. No one was informed of the motivation for this interview, so I answered the questions about my religious beliefs and social ideas honestly. During the interview, they also incomprehensibly stated they would be reworking all future curriculum to include teaching the gospel through the use of Disney characters. The interviewer looked honestly surprised when I responded incredulously. The whole thing was irritating and invasive, so I wasn't thinking about what I was saying or to whom.

My mom used to be the director at this school and had quit a couple of years before, screwed by its looming tightness. She kept telling me I had to get out of there, but I felt close to particular kids and didn't want to leave.

There was another woman on the staff named Norma. Norma was comically aggressive in her evangelism and reliably disagreeable. While she wasn't mean to the children, she wasn't even remotely warm. Her frog face was huge, and her eyes were startlingly bugged out. She had a terrible temper and lost her shit a lot. Even when she was calm, her face made it look like she was flipping out. Norma's whole thing as a human was difficult to take seriously. During lunch, she ate fruit flies and gnats with a long chaste tongue.

I was supposed to lock up the school after six and make sure everyone was out. Norma was still there, working on a bulletin board or something, and I told her, as she well knew, that she had to split. She ignored me and kept on working. Part of me knew it was a terrible idea to get into it with her, and part of me had to close the fucking school. I told her I really needed to leave and so did she. She still didn't respond. I have no idea why I said something so idiotic, but I said, "Hey, take the cotton out of your ears! The school is closed. We gotta go!"

She pushed past me and careened toward the church office, which was open until 7:30. I called my boss, Marta, and told her what was going on. She exhaled loudly and thought for a second and then told me to just let her do her thing and forget about it, but she sounded very worried—more worried than made sense to me. I was pissed, though, and as an irrational hothead, I followed Norma to the office, assuming she was going to complain about me to the pastor, who, although not involved in any day-to-day school activity, was the de facto head administrator, as is unfortunately the case at most small private schools. I found her in the copy room taking deep breaths and I bizarrely repeated the rickety "cotton in your ears" line.

She gasped and shoved her finger in my face and whisper-shouted, "I know what you are! I know what you do, and soon you are going to pay for it!"

I was stunned for a moment and then didn't care any-more, so I walked away. I got on my bike, rode to the train, and went home. I really doubted she knew I was bi or that I drank, so what did she know? That I didn't take the Bible literally? She might have known that I played in bands, but I couldn't imagine she had any idea what kind of music we made. Obviously, something was up, and for the first time, all the warnings I'd been given to leave the school were feel-ing ominous rather than insulting. The next day, there was a yogurt cup with a lid on it in the middle of my desk. I thought maybe a child or one of the parents had left it there as a little gift. When I opened it, it was filled to the top with huge slugs. I chucked it out the window.

A week later I was informed that the pastor, Pastor Gucci, wanted to talk to me and that it was not going to be good. I asked Marta what it was about and she wouldn't tell me. I was subbing for someone with an early shift, so this was at 8 a.m. I had the whole day to get worked up about it. By the time the children were taking their naps at noon, I was having a fit. Marta put her face to the chicken-wire window in the door of the classroom I was in. I pointed at her, picked the little table I was eating lunch at about an inch off the floor, and slammed it down. I was freaking out. The job and students that meant so much to me were going to go away.

My boss came back about ten minutes later. The children were still asleep, and she told me to go to the pastor's office now. The only other time he and I had talked was when I'd had a car accident right outside of the school parking lot. I'd had a little cut on my head but wasn't really hurt, though my car was totaled. I was supposed to meet a friend who was having a bad time a couple miles down the street, and he'd offered to drive me there. We were meeting at a bookstore to talk. When I told him where to drop me off he said, "A bookstore? What kind of books?" He drove a big, black new Audi. No other pastor I'd ever met drove anything new, let alone a big, black Audi. He didn't talk to me in the car but prayed before we drove, and when I reached out to shake his hand and say thanks, he waited a little too long before shaking it and looked over my head while he did it. His hand felt like a rag. He acted like a rag.

When I got to his office, he wasted no time telling me that at the marketing interview, it was determined I was "not Christian enough" and that I was being let go. They would give me a good reference, but they would need my keys that night. I started to cry and tried to explain to him how devoted I was to the children and that I was, in fact, a Christian. He said it "did not matter what I thought."

Something in me had no intention of giving up. He and I went back and forth for an hour arguing about theology and spirituality. He told me I was a danger to the children and that I threw furniture and that playing non-Christian music was an affront to God. At one point, I tried to pray with him that the school board would change their minds about me and realize that God knew I was committed to the families at the school. I was crying the whole time, and he was getting impatient and making a big corporate-tycoon show of loosening his tie.

Despite being in control while he was speaking, his face was turning pink, and he was starting to sweat. He told me there was one thing I could do to keep my job. I told him I would do anything. He told me to come over to his side of the desk and kneel; I figured it was to do some autocratic, whacked-out, evangelical BS. But his pants were already down around his ankles, and the dick we have all been waiting for was out and stiff. He told me to put it in my mouth.

I stood, walked to the door, and tried to open it, but it was locked from the inside. He said, as they all do, "No one will believe you." I heard a click and turned to see him holding a remote control, and the door opened.

In the hallway, one of the secretaries, who in her former life worked for the Marcos regime in the Philippines, handed me my last check. It was for about two hundred dollars more than it should have been. That was a lot of money for me at the time. The secretary asked for my keys, and my hand was shaking so much, I dropped them on the ground so she had to bend down to pick them up. She looked at me like I did it on purpose.

I walked across the parking lot back to the school to get my stuff. There was a box in the main office that had all the parents' emergency contact information in it. This was before everything was duplicated digitally, so these were the only copies. The law says that a school has to have emergency contacts on hand at all times, for a lot of good reasons. I thought about taking the box with me just to fuck with them because it would be a colossal pain in the ass to get all the information again, and they would be fined if there was an inspection and they didn't have it. But a couple of people on the staff really cared about the students, and I didn't want to make things hard for them. The rest of the employees were former crystal meth dealer biker ol' ladies who rationalized every shitty thing they ever did and then swung real hard in the other direction toward inflexible dogmatism to fool themselves that they were making up for it.

Marta had a smiling school-day portrait of herself taped to her desk phone. I turned it upside down and went into my now-empty classroom to look at it for the last time. They'd timed things so I couldn't say goodbye to the students, which made me feel monumentally sad. I wouldn't have wanted them to see me so upset, but it was incredibly rotten-hearted that the administration would choose to confuse the children so much. For many of them, we had been in a class together for six to eight hours a day for most of their tiny lives.

A year and half after all this, by some miracle, I started to make a living as a musician, for which I will be eternally grateful, but there was absolutely no indication then that things were going to work out. This job was everything.

My bicycle was in the main office, so I had to go back in there again to get away. The photo of Marta was turned right side up; she must have done it. I took a black Sharpie and drew a line across her eyes and turned it upside down again. Out of all the people there, she could have and should have helped me and didn't. I left her a venomous, no-turning-back note in all-caps red ink on her desk that, to this day, I wish I had signed with 666.

It started to rain, and although I was crying, I thought that it was a little funny. I had been riding my bike to work for three years, and I'd never gotten caught out in the rain until that day. Oh tears and oh drops of cloud's milk, oh cows in clouds! My sodden dignity and my sodden delusions falling as one upon my swollen face! I rented *Princess Mononoke* and ate white toast with olive oil in my housemate's bedroom. My VCR was broken, and he wasn't home.

Marta must have called my mom, because my sister knew that I'd gotten fired and told me to come over. I couldn't stop crying but I went over there, and she and her new fiancé, who was a friend of mine, were making a pot of mead. We had a tradition of trying new drinks together. I imagined that there were big mustard colored honey ants walking around the bottom of the pot as they cooked it. I told my sister everything, except for Pastor Gucci's dick, which I never told anyone about for, like, fifteen years. It didn't upset me, and it wasn't the worst thing about this situation in any way. He was a stupid person that I never took seriously, and it wasn't as if I'd trusted or believed in his character, so it didn't feel like that much of a violation. His dick in my face was just one more fucking thing on the place's list of soulless official and unofficial hypocrisies. Clearly I didn't forget about it, so perhaps somewhere deep inside me, this added to the other mounds of nonsense that I've decided make me a bad person sometimes and that's why I never told anyone, but copingly, I just don't think it was that big a deal. The person I did finally talk to was my best friend, while we were on a long drive. She's had to deal with more than her fair share of unasked-for dicks in her face, so I expected she might have an informed perspective. She asked me how I felt about it, and when I told her, she just laughed and then commented on a beautiful row of eucalyptus trees in the distance.

I could not, however, get over losing this job. It hurt me in a profound way. There were students there that I had seen every day for four years, and I missed them very, very much. At night, I lay awake and thought about how to get back at the school. I wanted to chop down a tree that was in the play yard, but that really would only bum the kids out and make too much noise.

Several months after I was fired, I took my housemate's truck at 1 a.m. and drove to the school. I knew they didn't bother to close any of the transom windows, which were always open about an inch and half between the frame and the building.

Behind Pastor Gucci's office was a little student vegetable garden with a hose. I put on gloves and threaded the hose through the space in the open window until I could see that it was touching the carpet. I turned the hose on all the way and left. If no one found it, and no one would have, water would have run into the building for about six hours until they opened the church office.

The church, elementary school, and preschool went bankrupt about a year later and closed down. The preschool had been floating the other offices for a decade, and when they changed the program to the freakish Disney thing, enrollment plummeted. When they were going over the bankruptcy accounting, they discovered that Pastor Gucci had been stealing money from all three institutions ever since he'd been hired. A private investigator also found that he was gambling, smoking, drinking, and cheating on his wife, which, for fundamentalists, is a huge deal. His wife, who I have to say was an almost visibly corroded person as well, left him, and he was defrocked. After he was convicted of embezzlement, he did twenty months in low security at FCI Lompoc.

A few years later, I was a volunteer for the Prisoners Literature Project. Whenever there was a request for books from people who were more than likely white supremacists, asking for Nordic or Celtic mythology, *Mein Kampf*, and blah blah blah, we would send them *The Autobiography of Malcolm X* or bell hooks as a joke. Whenever we got a letter from Lompoc, I daydreamed about what books I could have sent Pastor Dick.

LUAN WU AND
IMELDA TANTOCO

For a while when I lived in San Jose, there were two people I was doing it with, Luan and Imelda. They didn't make any promises to me and I didn't make any to them. There were unspoken assumptions that I knew they had, but as they remained unspoken, I did whatever I wanted. They didn't know about each other until they did. I don't know how they found out, but I was pretty cavalier about being whorish, so it was inevitable.

They were unhappy about my bullshit, and the way they got back at me—and I can think of this having happened in no other way than by some kind of foggy-night, trench-coated coordination—was and is worthy of my eternal Fuck You, Jamie Stewart respect and consideration. On a Wednesday evening, only minutes apart, they each, in turn, called to say that they did not want to sleep with me anymore. They didn't mention why. This made me feel like a jerk, and it made me tense.

They knew that I had certain habits and that every Thursday after work, I ate dinner at a tiny Indian restaurant in a hallway at the back of an Indian grocery store. I had taken Luan and Imelda there separately on a lot of Thursdays.

When I arrived, as I regularly would, the day after they both called me, I found them both sitting at a table with two friends of mine, Seaman and Bam Bam. These were guys that I played music with sometimes, and we had just been in the middle of rehearsing to go on a long tour. They were kind of scummy, but they were also taller and younger than me, and they dressed more thoughtfully. Seaman has remained scummy. Bam Bam is really cool now.

Luan was sitting close to Seaman, one of her hands way up his thigh and the other up his shirt. Imelda was sitting next to Bam Bam. Her head was perched on his shoulder and her lips were touching his neck. All four smelled of worldly jizz and had bedhead. They waved me over but didn't say anything.

What else could I do but sit with them? They all wore shit-eating grins and had just finished their food. I sat on a milk crate at the corner edge of their four-person table.

"Hey, Seaman, how big is your dick?" I asked.

"Um, it's pretty big," he said in a quiet, high voice, looking away.

"Yeah, you're tall. Hey, Bam Bam, how big is your dick?"

"Oh, it's pretty, um, big too," he said, trying to maintain his inane expression.

"Mine is just pretty normal," I said.

Luan looked at me with her mouth open, and Imelda called me an asshole. I picked up their check and left.

Imelda and I had met at a concert I played at UC Berkeley that she and some other students had put together. After the show, she, a couple friends of hers, a bandmate of mine named Otto, and I went to get ice cream. Next to the ice cream place was a sex store. We all went in and looked at impossible-to-stuff-in fuck toys, deep and rarefied fetish DVDs, and a heroic world of shining bondage equipment, which included a vinyl lion-tamer getup. Imelda was the only one not laughing, and she handled each dangling item analytically, with what appeared to be genuine, straight-faced interest. She was more striking than traditionally pretty, had a cool 1957 pinup's figure and style, and was smart. While we were chatting, she said she was a microbiology research major. Otto, a smarty-pants and unabashed nerd himself, imploded at hearing a real, live girl say this between the walls of a clean and well-lit place for rubber cocks. He slipped out the door to jack off into the bushes and, when he came back, said it was "a funny night."

Having gotten my number from whoever put the show together, Imelda called me about a week later, and we started to talk pretty regularly. She was absorbingly and openly idiosyncratic and lost her patience with my being elusive when she asked personal questions. To keep her from hanging up, I usually ended up saying more than I should have, but that would lead to her telling me too much also.

Valentine's Day was coming and we were both single, so we decided to get dinner in Berkeley. It was incredibly awkward, and whatever perceived confidence she had on the phone, she did not have in person. Despite not wanting to admit it to myself, it became clear that she thought we were dating. I was fond of her but didn't want this to be more than just pals who overconfided, which was, to say the least, dim, as it was Valentine's Day. She told me flat-out that I would pay for dinner.

After we left, we went for a walk around downtown, and she told me at least three times that she was a virgin. I finally understood that she wanted to lose this virginity this very tonite. She was twenty-one and a junior in college. We went to her campus apartment, where an experimental forest of pustule-and-cyst roommates gloomed at us from in front of a sci-fi marathon on the television. Her room was cluttered but clean. It was the sort of student room that looked very much like a student lived there.

Imelda told me to turn around, and she changed into a mortifyingly formal white silk dressing gown with a long matching slip and large hair bow. It was mortifying because it looked like it belonged to her grandmother; she must have thought it looked wonderful and that she was taking our romance very seriously. She lit several candles and we sat on the bed and started to kiss. I kept thinking about Miss Havisham.

When I was eighteen and twenty, I had two other girl-friends who were virgins, but I wasn't eighteen or twenty anymore. Part of me felt yucky to be doing this without really talking to her about it ahead of time, part of me felt flattered to have been conscripted for this bedazzled night, and part of me felt glad to be having any kind of sex at all, even macabre sex.

It started slowly, but it became apparent that she had been wanting to get fucked for a long time. She was groaning and grinding like a demon, and I was kind of taken aback. She didn't have the moves or technique of a sexually experienced person, but she had the will. All her flowing white clothes were still on and, in the same way she'd wanted me to pay for dinner, she wanted me to remove them. The rotten part of me wanted to leave the bow on, but I carefully took both it and her robe off. This made her go wild and she leapt on top of me, trying very hard but struggling to pull my pants and shirt off. Her roommates started yelling "Yuck!" through the door because of the sounds, but she didn't care.

She grabbed at my cock through my panties but was unintentionally too rough, so I slid off the bed onto my knees and spread her legs apart to go down on her. The panties she was wearing matched the rest of her outfit: they were too big, slightly worn, and also white silk. I took them off and kissed her all over down there. Her pussy was dainty and tasted good. She really, really, really liked getting head and made intense grunts. After a long time, she started whimpering, "Now, now, now . . . " so I slid my cock inside of her. It got very quiet and I could tell it hurt her a lot, but I could also tell she knew it would and so was concentrating and inhaling through it. There were academic and Kiwanis Club ribbons and medals all over one section of the wall. I could see an illuminated certificate of achievement emerge from behind her sweaty forehead and float across the room to join them. The white slip was still on, bunched up above her hips.

We didn't talk about protection, so I didn't want to cum, and I was also going really slowly and it would have taken forever. There was no blood. When I pulled out, we kept touching and licking. She was moving a little more stiffly but was still horned up.

Not being sure we would ever hook up again and not feeling bad about maybe being used to just fucking get this over with, I sportingly attempted a wide range of additional activities. I sucked her toes, had her watch me jack off, gave her ass a long massage, and started to give her a rim job while she was on all fours. As I was licking her out and she was responding with characteristic vigor, the long buildup of the night caught me, and I shot cum all over the backs of her calves. She looked over her shoulder at me with an expression of what could only be called wonder.

I wanted to go home really badly but knew I had to spend the night. It was hard to sleep in her tiny bed, and we both woke up tired and crabby. She gave me some water in the morning but didn't walk me to my car. We never defined our relationship, and over the next two years, we fucked on and off a few times a month. Once in a while we got hot chocolate or something, but usually we just fucked. Mostly, I treated her even less than dismissively. When I ran into her about five years after we'd stopped seeing each other, she turned her back to me in the middle of my asking her how she'd been, walking away with two middle fingers up over her shoulders.

A couple of weeks into our hanging out, we went to the movies and she asked me to jerk her off in the theater. When we got back to my room, she wanted me to fuck her standing up against the wall while she talked in a little girl's voice about how badly behaved she was while I pretended to be her schoolteacher. Then she told me to pull her hair and cum on her face. As far as I knew, this was the third time she had ever had sex in her life. She is the only person who has ever asked me to cum on their face.

For a long time, she didn't have a car and took the bus from Berkeley to meet up. It took way more than an hour to get to my house. I told her first thing in the morning—or, just as often, right after we finished messing around at night—that I needed her to leave because I was busy. I thought or didn't think that not being nice would make it clear I wasn't a boyfriend. I never talked with her about it. I don't know what my fucking problem was, or why I treated her so badly, because she was never mean to me.

Over the summer, she was home with her parents near San Luis Obispo, and we decided to meet at a motel in central California. I was driving to LA to see a friend and play accordion badly in his questionable band. We had talked on the phone about doing anal and she told me, "Well, what if I don't want to do it?" and I said, trying to act like a top, "You want what I want." She giggled, which she never did, and said, "I don't think you can handle it."

We messed around at the motel for a long time. There was a clicky ballpoint pen on the nightstand. I put it in Imelda's hand and had her insert it into my urethra. Her eyes got really big and then I had her turn around and sit on my face so I could lick out her ass while she fucked the pen in and out of my little slit.

When I started to push my dick against her butthole and slid it in, she stared at my face like she was looking at a newborn mandrill—with pity, adoration, and queasy disgust. When I was close, I asked her where she wanted me to cum and she said she didn't care, just to hurry up and do it. The second after I came in her ass, she jumped up and went into the restroom.

We lay around in the motel for a little bit, and then I got up to get dressed and get ready to finish the drive to my friend's house. She looked hurt that I was leaving and asked me in a childish, played-up voice, "Do you want to go out and wander?"

I said to her in a fake cowboy voice, "I gotta go, little lady," and we looked down at the bedsheets.

After she graduated, she moved to San Jose and got a job working on the genome project. I told her I thought this was possibly immoral and gave her a book about genetic engineering and the end of humanity for her birthday. She then fucked one of my roommates, who was really ugly, and they both unconvincingly denied it. He also stole and then sold some music equipment of mine that was in our shared living room. Then, while he was on tour, someone stole the entire trailer filled with his band's amps and guitars right off the back of his van. I had nothing to do with that, but I felt it made us even.

Imelda and I kept seeing each other semiregularly and kept not defining what our thing was. I told her that her vagina felt memorable and that its sensation was distinct. She said thank you. She told me that she liked to fuck me when I was drunk because I was better and wilder than when I was sober. I pretended that this didn't bother me because I didn't want her to have the upper hand. That night, I felt I needed to impress her to maintain my position, so I cut off tiny snips of her and my hair and ate them while we were doing it. On my nightstand I had a rainbow-colored NASCAR mag flashlight and fucked that into her while I put a little pink egg vibrator on her clit. Then I lubed up and put my cock in her ass. A little feces got on the sheet, and I made a big deal about having to wash it. She was silent.

She started to make OK money at her job and moved into a decent apartment, got a car, and told me she wanted to get me a Swatch watch. She never did, but I bought one for myself and told friends she got it for me. I pretended like I was being kept, but really I did it so that people would think someone liked me enough to buy me something. The band I play in almost named our first record *I'll Buy You That* based on this watch thing. The person who played drums on it told me it was a wasteful title, which is not untrue.

Imelda invited me over to her new place to play video games and watch *The Piano Teacher*. I went to the ninety-nine-cent store and bought a bunch of rubber snakes and a cheap vase so I could give her a rubber-snake bouquet. I meant it as a nothing housewarming present, but she was incredibly excited and genuinely appreciative. It made me feel like a shit, that a crappy present was all it took to make her feel some affection from me.

Luan and I met when I saw her playing cornet in an acquaintance's band. She had an appealingly unusual face but kind of a ridiculous hairdo. The sound was really terrible, so you couldn't hear her, but I figured it wasn't an instrument that someone who couldn't play would play. I asked her if she wanted to come over to do some recording on my little home studio setup. She didn't seem enthusiastic at first but eventually made it over. When she got there, it was pretty clear she sucked; we never used her parts, but it was still fun. We got along OK. She sat close to me and we had a good time talking. I asked her if she wanted to make out. She looked very surprised and said no, but then, after a minute, kissed me. I started to take off her clothes, but she made it very clear she wasn't into it, so we stopped and she left. About twenty minutes later, she came back and we fucked. She had a very nice body; she was short and really tight.

It didn't occur to me how Imelda might feel. It didn't occur to me how Luan might feel. I started to see both of them—Luan three or four times a week and Imelda our usual five or six times a month. Being a brute despite being socially incompetent, I was also having a lot of random one-night stands. For about nine months, I was having sex every day and often more than once a day with different people. There was one twenty-four-hour period from one noon to the next noon where I fucked one boy and three girls—though not at the same time. No one's feelings crossed my mind. It never crossed my mind that this was way more people to be fucking than was normal. It was fine, and it's funny to be able to describe nine months of life with the single word *fuckathon*, but I don't look back at it with any great delight. It feels shameful or blankly functional—not shameful for all the sex but for the famished, crablike disregard with which I treated most of the people involved. (Not that I am wildly successful now, but a few cool things have happened that act as a buffer against total despair.) Back then, my existence bordered on being an unlivable nightmare, and nothing lastingly cool enough to make this nightmare less unmanageable ever happened, except for constantly getting laid. An overexposure to sex throughout my life and being abused as a kid made it more necessary, too, than I realized, I'm sure. Hopefully now I would be able to be nice to the models of and even enjoy a renewed nine-month subscription to *The Fuckathon Redux:*

117

Real-Life Willing Holes, but I know it is an accomplishment or fate I would never be able to purposely reignite. Whatever pink magic that makes that kind of mindless consumption possible will always ignore any conscious attempt to control it.

Luan worked part-time at a copy shop and took community college art student-caliber photos. She lived with her parents and was saving up money to backpack around Asia and generally trying to figure it out. Sex with her was less fraught and intense than it could be with Imelda, and less creative, but it was still good. She made a lot of loud noises, and when I would cum on her stomach, she would rub it violently all over her tits and throat, running her tongue across her teeth. We tried anal once, but after about ten seconds, and with an informed and totally certain look on her face, she shouted, "Out! Out! Out! This is not right!" Other than that, we had an unweird and unepic but quality time in bed. Her tightness and overall enthusiasm went a long way.

The main drag about her was that she, while bright, was a little slow on the uptake while being too quick emotionally. After a couple weeks of dating, she began a ritual of writing me seven- to ten-page letters almost every day about not very much. It was nice, but we talked on the phone all the time and only lived about fifteen minutes away from each other. After a bit, the letters started to build up, and I stopped opening them. A huge pile of them bred in my dresser drawer. I told this to my mom. She sighed and said that I at least had to open them in case Luan ever went through my stuff. I grabbed a pair of scissors and sliced the tops open so it would be obvious they weren't still sealed. My mom's advice was good because the next week, Luan was looking for a T-shirt and found them. She gave me a look that said *Oh, you saved them all . . .*

Her unserious college and work schedule allowed her to come over between classes. One day, she arrived with a gigantic women's studies textbook. I said she should let me spank her with it. "C'mon! It would be dumb!" I think her developing a social consciousness was still really new and therefore still really grave, and she looked at me like I'd told her to release an enema all over her grandfather's childhood drawings from the War. She said she was mad and sat in the corner, not talking to me. After ten minutes, she blurted out that she wanted me to start calling her "Dhiah." I told her it sounded like diarrhea and that I couldn't do it. Now even more mad, she threw a chapbook of photographed self-portraits at me that she had brought over as a gift. The photos were of her wrapped in crinoline, her hands in mudra poses or nudes of her in "tribal" face paint.

A few weeks later, lying face-to-face on our sides and steadily balling, my cock inside of her, she looked me dead in the eye and started to sing a Bright Eyes song. I stopped moving, completely unsure of what had happened to reality. There's something laudable about being so vulnerable, and there's also something outrageously repulsive about it. I liked her, though, and wanted to keep things going on, so I did everything I could to try not to make her feel embarrassed. But also—NO FUCKING WAY.

Her birthday was the following week. I went to a medical supply store and got her a folding white cane, the kind people who are visually impaired use. I thought it was just

119

an interesting human object and a cool present. She became livid and told me that because I never told her that I loved her back, this present was a way of calling her blind. I asked her when it was that she'd told me she loved me, terrified that I'd somehow forgotten. Luan sat in the corner with a clamped mouth and scowled at me like a tubby white cop with a mustache. After ten minutes of tense silence, she stood up, took off my clothes without another word, and (in comparison to her usual, less fervent mode) fucked the fuck out of me. I tried to spank her with the cane—was there ever any question I wouldn't have?

I didn't know she had told me she was in love with me because this declaration was in one of the hundreds of millions of letters she'd sent. It must have sucked, waiting for me to say it back or at least acknowledge it at all. Luan never brought up love again. I remained unaware of the contents of this letter until after we stopped seeing each other, when, possessed by a drunken and heartless curiosity, I finally went through them all.

The next time I saw her, she was wearing silver-and-copper snakeskin pants. I thought she was wearing them ironically and I said something like, "Whoa, dude!"

She brightened and said, "Thank you! Aren't they awesome?" and then I knew she meant it. I told my sister about the pants, and she told me I really needed to break up with her. Not long after this I got their synchronized breakup calls.

About two months later, my dad committed suicide. Luan, even though we weren't talking at that point, tried a bunch of times to get me to let her be there for me. I kept turning her away and was being really cold about it. Later, when the suicidal dust settled, I left a message and tried to say sorry and thank you, but the suicidal dust had settled for her, too, and she ignored me and has since.

There is a large secret laboratory and observation post beneath a not-great goth club in San Jose called Studio 8. Imelda and Luan share a cubicle, bench, and stainless-steel work table there, fitted with video monitors that are able to look both forward and backward into space and time. There are an endless number of colored pens and composition books with mottled burgundy-and-cream covers neatly stacked under the table and against the gray fabric walls. They each use one color of ink for recording the misgivings and humiliations of the future and a different color for recording the misgivings and humiliations of the past. Imelda uses a black Edding 1200 Superior Quality felt-tip for the future and a red Uni-Ball Vision Fine for the past. They both leak ink on her fingers. Luan, somewhat savagely, uses an orange bold-point Sharpie for the future but then, conversely, a demure Pilot Kakuno disposable fountain pen in green for the past.

The writing hurts their eyes when they proofread their notes because the lighting is bad, and then also because of the ink's colors, obviously.

They don't use the rest of the lab's equipment, but other people do.

THE CLAREMONT

There was a strip club in Atlanta that shared a building with a halfway house. It might not be there anymore, but it probably is. Women who live in the halfway house also work at the club. The dancers there have lives and bodies you don't normally see naked on a stage. I've never been there without something ludicrous happening.

We played an early show, so the rest of the night was free. The other bands on the tour wanted to have some fun and the Claremont blew its Mr. Clarinet. As we entered, there was a woman on the stage named Hamburger Mary who weighed five hundred pounds. The stage was very small and placed above and behind the bar. It was round and surrounded by all the bottles of booze with the bartender standing right in front of it, so the dancers didn't have a lot of space to do their thing. Because of her size, Hamburger Mary had even less. She slid and rippled unevenly to the music; it was mesmerizing and lawless. Astounded smirks all around the room, everyone's id unraveled to the bedlam of curious pain and bad news.

It was the first tour that I ever made a little money. This was a new experience and I didn't know what to do with it, so I crammed it all into the front zipper pocket of my pullover windbreaker. When I wore it, the ball of money made me look like I was stealing a roll of paper towels. As my friends were settling in, I was possessed by a need to count this money. This happens on low-rent tours as your mind starts to fatigue. You need some tactile reinforcement and a quantified reminder that the days going by have an end and a purpose.

In the corner of the club was a young muscle guy, obviously on angel dust, grabbing the back of a chair over and over and slamming it down. I'd seen him there before, working as a bouncer, but he just seemed to be a customer that night. We sat as far from him as we could, and I decided to go hide in the kitchen to count my loot, thinking no one could see me. This was next-level naïve. As I was laying out the bills across the top of a chest freezer, I heard the breathing of the elephant smasher. Angel-dust dude had followed me back there.

"I could fucking kill you right now." His eyes were half-open and goggling in circles.

"I'm sure you could."

"I like that money, and I like to kill, and I could kill you easily."

I felt like I'd been caught cheap-eating sweet-and-sour pork over a sink filled with abattoir urine. The guy screamed a high-pitched scream in my face and then started screech-cackling. Time had stopped and my mind had stopped. Next he grabbed a twenty-dollar bill, lit it with a lighter, and then waved it in front of his eyes for a long time. He walked out of the kitchen, led by the flame. By now my sleep-deprived dim-wittedness was quite cleared away and I ran back to my friend's tables, thanking God.

The stage was now owned by a curvy, natural looking blond woman with an arm that stopped at the elbow. She was somehow conducting a wider grind than the little stage was made to accommodate. It was impressive. We all clapped and cheered. We ordered drinks, relaxed a little, and started to talk.

After about ten minutes, we heard crashing and shouting and turned to see the angel-dust guy standing on the bar, grabbing the leg of the blond dancer and punching her in the breasts. The bartender was waving a baseball bat in his face and the bouncer who was actually working the door that night was yelling, "Marcus! Stop! Marcus! Stop!" The dancer was trying not to fall onto the bottles each time she was punched. As if flicked behind the ear by the demon that was controlling him, Marcus let her go, leapt high off the bar, and ran out the door.

This event hardly disrupted the night at all, and after thirty seconds of "Whoa, that was crazy," people went back to what they were doing before. The music never stopped playing, the bartender helped the beat-on dancer get down from the stage, and the bouncer resumed sitting on his stool by the door. Up next was a woman who was severely anorexic, junked out, and wearing an Elvira wig that was way loose and too big for her head.

The bass player in one of the bands we were on tour with was an exotic dancer for her day job and had more insight into the place than the rest of us. She was, of course, totally in love with it and buying well drinks for all to celebrate the other side of the looking glass. At this time, I usually only drank beer or wine and didn't have a clear sense of what six or seven shots right after each other might mean. My guts began to wobble as undead, and I sensed a new lurking disobedience inside me.

Over the music, we heard the karaoke machine turn on and a horror-show voice start singing an Alice in Chains song. Marcus had come back in. He was holding the mic in his fist like a hammer, and no one did anything. There were two parallel universes in that club, one stacked on top of the other and both stacked on the edge. The dancer danced her awful dance in her Baphomet wig and the singer sang his awful song in his Baphomet voice. When he was done, he ran out the door again. The bartender waited a minute and then put his bat down behind the bar while the bouncer carried the offensive machine away.

As part of her recognition of the night's black chalice, the bass-playing woman getting us too drunk decided I needed a lap dance. I could neither accept nor refuse. I saw her talking to a dancer and then pointing at me. From across the room, I could see the dancer was tall with long brown hair and was wearing a garter belt, stockings, and panties, but she was naked other than that. I was too faded to feel aroused but also faded enough to feel philosophical and bemused. My friend was smiling a huge smile. Two cigarettes were hanging out of her mouth as she watched the dancer straddle me and squish down on my lap.

The dancer's face had been severely burned. She had almost no nose—just two holes, no upper lip, and one eye that was almost completely grown-over with wrinkled skin. Her body was very nice. I found out later that she was called "the Fifty-Foot Fakeout"; from far away she looked great, etc.

A song she liked came on and she shimmied a professional, excited shimmy. Her arms were around my neck and her body was pressed into my face. The room began to spin, and I threw up all over her tits.

"Oh my God, I am so sorry," I said. "It's not you. It's not you."

She looked at me with no expression. "Give me fifty dollars," she croaked. I handed it over.

The bouncer was standing next to us by now and seemed jaded out of his mind. He grabbed me by the back of my collar, chucked me out the door, and then yawned. My friends followed, laughing so hard that two of them were lying on the pavement in the parking lot.

The bounce man said quietly, "Please get out of here." We drove to the punk house where all eight of us were going to sleep. When I got there, someone handed me a plastic gas-station bottle labeled 99 PROOF BUTTERSCOTCH, restrained both my hands, and lifted the container to my mouth. I began to shake and then could not see. Part of me remembers lying in a bathtub, retching to blackout and being doused with water and endless streams of dusty mucus pouring out my nose. The woman who invited us to sleep at the house was apparitionaly hovering over the tub to keep me from choking and lifting my head to the faucet so I could drink water and cool down.

I was wearing a shirt from one of the bands we were on tour with and took it off to swab the mucus from my face. It was all in my eyes and mouth. This band was particularly twee, and the shirt was pink with a little computer drawn on it, in every way perfect for the job.

When I woke up, I was facedown on the porch outside on a layer of old towels. I had shit and pissed in my pants, and no one wanted to deal with it. I was soaking wet with sweat from my gross body, dew from the morning's rebirth, and holy water from the bathtub of life. My guardian angel was asleep in a deck chair and woke up when I did.

"You had real bad alcohol poisoning, and I didn't want to be known as the lady who killed your band," she said. This woman who kept me from dying later went on to become the tour manager for Huey Lewis and the News. We still talk occasionally.

The shirt that I used to wipe the snot from my face had been tossed onto the grass and transformed into a crawling, sapient clot. I took off my remaining clothes, put them in the trash, and stood naked in the yard, using a hose to clean myself. Convulsing from this cold shower and the yucky party still inside me, I took the bottom towel that had none of my shit on it, dried off, and slept in the van.

The singer from the band whose shirt was left on the grass found it there. He was very tall and heavy, and I had a flash of memory seeing him fucking a girl on top of a row of couch cushions on the floor. His ass was like a casserole pan with two halves of a hairy cantaloupe glued to it. He washed the shirt off and sold it at his merch table like regular.

PIZZA LADY

Seattle is a depressing city. Any place that has a moment and then sees that moment fade is depressing: Detroit, Memphis, San Francisco. Seattle is small, too, and you can walk everywhere, which is good because there's not a lot else to do there except drink and wring out your mop of fucking tears.

I moved there after living in a warehouse in Oakland. In the early 2000s, this was a not uncommon—though, I am sure, totally illegal—living situation. Downstairs was AK Press and next door was a dildo factory. The factory only made dildos in the shape of religious figures: God the Father, the Grim Reaper, Abraham, Vishnu, Jesus, et al. Their products were awfully big, as I suppose was only appropriate. There was a wheelbarrow next to the entrance where they chucked all the defects. Half-melted gods piled upon discolored prophets. Whenever a new someone moved into the warehouse, they always grabbed a few to decorate their frantically cordoned space. Every person who lived in that clapboard warren had a row of defective blasphemy dicks on their windowsill (if they had a window) or nightstand (made of a milk crate). I had one of the Grim Reaper ones. The one time I tried to use it on someone, he immediately yelled, "Take it out, take it out!"

It's not as rough now, but at that point, the neighborhood was incredibly bad; there were lots of gangs, drugs, and street prostitution. I was mostly too dense to know how dangerous it was. Luckily, the worst thing that happened to me was that one night someone stole one of the headlights out of my minivan. Then, two days later, they stole the other one. I was too broke to go to the dealership to replace them and found a pair at a junkyard. When I installed them, I did it wrong, and they pointed down so that only five feet in front of the van was illuminated. This also seemed only appropriate.

A couple years shy of thirty, I started an unsuitable relationship with a nineteen-year-old named Lois who lived in Seattle and was even crazier than I was. Her life was only pain and my life was only pain. She was an acquaintance of a couple of people I knew from the early days of touring. They'd offered to sort out an art gallery where my bandmates and I could set up to work on a record if we wanted to drive up to Seattle. We were getting to be friends and talked about them playing on the record with us too. Both of these guys were crashing either on the couch or in a copper 1980s Toyota van parked in front of a house called Clown Town. Neither of them lived there, but they said we could stay there too. It was unclear if they'd asked the people who really did live there about this, Lois being one of them. For some convoluted logistical reason, I drove up alone, and my other two bandmates came a day later. We regrouped, got started on the record with our friends, and slept on the hallway floor in sleeping bags as uninvited guests.

The last night we were going to be up there, the actual residents of the house happened to be having a party. I had a hard time having fun as a teenager. To rebel against the pandemonium of my home life, I focused on being uptight, doing my schoolwork, and being organized. As I got a little older, the energy that is in all young people decided it was time to start coming out. Mega Man Mayhem was the form it chose.

I got wasted at this party, making out with anyone, stripping down to my underwear and stuffing it with bedsheets so my balls looked pregnant, and conjuring clouds of blood and ravenously grasping for that lost time. What a feeling, dancing on the ceiling. One of my bandmates worked nights, so 11 p.m. for him was like eight in the morning for most people. Being overly familiar with the smeared and various stages of my devolving state, and in order to keep from having to deal with me and them, he and my other bandmate drove home without saying anything. Just before the sun was coming up and the party was fading, Lois, also wasted, led me by the hand into her tiny, windowless basement room. She whispered in my ear, "Wanna fuck?" Afterward, we were both surprised by our connection, I think. She started laughing and then purposely peed in bed while we lay on our backs, holding hands. I went back to Oakland that night, and we started talking on the phone every day. Too soon, I told her everything I was feeling, and too soon, I meant it.

A month later, Lois came to visit. She took a Greyhound all the way down, and while I was waiting for her to arrive after work, I snuck into a house where I used to live to take a nervous dump and clean it off in the shower. It didn't all come out when I was on the toilet and I shit more onto the shower tile when I was washing my hole. It took a long time to force it down the drain. When I arrived at the depot, out of the corner of my eye I saw a willow reed lurch on a pair of low-cost, very red, very high heels and I hoped it wasn't her, but it was.

We had a nice time, though—no good in life otherwise—and thought, *Fuck it.* I quit my job with no notice, left my "apartment" with no notice, shaved my head down to the skin, and, from one frying-pan slum into another of flame, drove us up the West Coast to her own flophouse eight hundred miles away.

To try and work out the Canopus in Argos of chaos inside me, I had been punching myself in the face a lot and had two black eyes and a big scab on the side of my nose. While picking up my last check, one of the teachers at the latest pre-school where I was working started laughing when I showed up like that, teasing me that I got my ass kicked. I told my coworker that my roommate's girlfriend was violent and that when she threw canned food at her, she ended up hitting me by accident. Written in lint or on smog was this poem:

Onward to Seattle, a corroded, gray-green minivan,
Crammed up and within the Joadian losers' tradition,
a skinhead with two black eyes
and a teenager with a wet cigarette's mind
only the risk of more sadness before them

Lois and I had a profoundly tearful, wounded breakup after about a year. Although I rarely think about it now, that breakup still crumples my heart. It took so long to close. We lived together for almost a whole additional year after it was over because we were both too broke to move out and find our own places. We also had to sleep in the same bed because our apartment was so small that there was nowhere else. We hugged through the nights, but we never had sex again. There was some love in there, but we were both too hardened to not make it awful. Lois was a pretty unlimited alcoholic and spent her time drunk on our mattress on the floor, watching television. The small water heater in the kitchen cabinet leaked and it seeped under the cheap laminate flooring; you could hear a *squish squish squish* when you stepped on it. The bottom of the bed was always soaked and covered with spots of black mold.

It was an unusually hot summer, we were broken up, and I was tired of being nothing to no one. I was going to go to a bar to be pitiful and get away from the moldy bed. We'd decided on a dating moratorium until we got our own places, but this wouldn't really be dating. I took a shower, shaved my area, and put on a new black dress shirt she'd bought me.

"I'm going to a bar."

"Are you going out to meet someone?"

"What? No! I just shaved because it's hot!"

"That shirt looks nice."

The bar was as dopey and crowded as possible. I pushed into the vague corner where I belonged and stood with a beer in each hand. I was wearing big headphones plugged into a blue Discman and trying to look any boy or girl in the eye.

In a short time, I gave in to the facts and was holding two new beers. A not-super-attractive, out-of-shape frat girl walked up to me, pulled off my headphones, and asked me if I was alone.

"In the flesh!" I said.

She was as drunk as one would think and shook her head at me sitting back down with her friends. After a few minutes, she walked up to the bartender and shout-slurred, "Hey, is that guy alone?" The bartender looked at me and laughed. In Seattle, every bartender is in a band that didn't go anywhere, so they're professional shitheads instead. Her friend waved me over to their table and yelled, "She wants you to go home with her."

We pounded our drinks, and she almost ran out the door. It was hard to keep up with her. Her little cube apartment was sincerely messy, and there were hockey and WNBA posters on the walls. Hugely taking up the one chair was a human-sized Alvin the Chipmunk doll.

She told me that I looked a lot older in the light. I felt embarrassed. There were no sheets on the bed and we got on it. She took off her pants and panties and I took off all my clothes. She had a perfectly hairless pussy, which was more unusual then than it is now. I told her how hot it was, and she put her finger to her lips and said in a rising tone, "Quiet! Quiet! QUIET!"

Her skin was axolotl pale and slithered with nebulas of blue and green veins. They weren't bumpy like varicose veins, but you could see them smooth and all over and under her Kleenex wrapping. She kind of sleepily sucked me off for thirty seconds and then pushed my head to her V-hole. Her bed was next to the fridge, and while I was trying to make something happen, she reached in, got out a frozen pizza, and started eating it. These two activities went on together for a little while and I was praying she wouldn't rest the pizza on top of my head. I sat up and, with her mouth full, she asked me if I came.

133

Pizza Lady went blind into her still-frozen pizza. I bundled up my clothes, quietly left, and got dressed in the hallway. The only thing that made sense, now and forever, was being more drunk.

Lois was still in bed watching TV and drinking beer when I got home. The sweat of the outside didn't make anything easier to forget. I took her beer out of her hand, drank it as fast as I could, and sat down on the damp floor, facing away from her.

TEEN COUPLE
BEFORE A SHOW

Not long after I moved to Seattle to live in the insane asylum of love Lois and I had built, I was asked to play a little house show in a little town in central Washington. This was before we had broken up. The place was about an hour and a half's drive from our cat box-sized apartment. I arrived at the house really early and the people who were living there were unprepared and annoyed for me to have shown up that far ahead of time, so I walked around the town, carrying my guitar like a dork.

A young-looking boy and girl on a scooter scooted up to me and asked if I was playing at that show. They said they were going to go and asked if I wanted to come over and hang out before. I had nothing else to do, so I went with them. They said they'd just graduated high school and moved in together about two months prior. Their place was brutally run-down, but it had a door and plumbing, so it was not uninhabitable. I cannot, to save my life, remember their names.

We stood in the chipping kitchenette, talking and listening to the Cure and Bauhaus. They were both pretty and nice, and neither was dim. The boy read as super gay, but she was all over him in the way that teenagers ravenously are, so there was something going on. She was wearing a paint-splattered men's button-up work shirt and, without my noticing, kept unbuttoning it until it was open past her bra.

She asked me if I wanted some tea, and she poured it into a cup with no handle that was shaped like a sweetie panda face. Before she handed it to me, she said I could only have it if she could watch me suck her boyfriend off. I laughed and they laughed, and then I said OK. Someone knocked on the front door, and they both started loudly howling like wolves. This must have been a thing they did a lot because they did it immediately and didn't look self-conscious when they were done. I thought for a second and said I would only do the deed if he used my head like a table to place the cup upon while he was in my mouth. They both went, "Ooooooooooooooh."

He pulled it out and had a good, not-too-big, not-too-small hard-on. I got down on my knees, and she got on her knees really close next to me to watch. Her shirt was totally open now and I could see she was wearing a wireless, light purple see-through bra and that her nipples were small, brown, and hard. They aimed at his cock. I put him into my mouth, and he tasted good.

I heard him pick up the cup from the counter, and when he placed it on my head, I started to laugh again because it was quite hot against my scalp. I had a buzz cut then, so there wasn't any hair to serve as a coaster. Laughing with a dick in your mouth makes you laugh more because you start to drool. They started laughing, too, and I was worried that he would spill hot tea on me, but he didn't. She was watching with her face right next to mine and I hoped she would get in on it, but she didn't. I didn't want to suggest anything because they were so little. The person I had moved up here for was little too. Passively cheating was bad enough, but to have *initiated* a cheat with someone even younger than my already-borderline problematically young love felt like even more of a betrayal than it would have been with someone more age-appropriate. It was too lecherous, too greedy, a breaking of our bond of wrongness.

Being a kid, he came really fast and big and luckily took the cup off my head before he finished, or I probably would have burned up and his dick probably would have gotten burned up too. I saw a gray mouse sitting on top of the bookshelf across the room, watching us. It made the *Ma perché?* gesture, grabbed its balls, and then scurried away to eat the binding glue from their books.

There was some cum on my mouth and chin, which she wiped away with her finger and then tapped into her lips like lip gloss. I really, really wanted to kiss it off her then, but you know . . .

As I stood up, we all started laughing again, and they said I could keep the panda cup. I told them I was going to ask for it anyway.

The boy and girl ended up not coming to the show, which I was not disappointed about., When I was trying to play, someone who lived there and didn't want a house show happening as they were trying to sleep or do their homework or live normally played the William S. Burroughs Thanksgiving poem real loud over and over to interrupt and protest. A decent move; it wasn't something I could hold against them. If I had a quicker mind, I would have accompanied rotten ol' Bill in a beatnik style—a paean to the older mouths of jagged skulls and the lightning jets of youth's inhumane glue.

DANIELLA DOS
SANTOS PEEBLES

If you drink real pulque, it feels like your consciousness starts floating six inches in front of your face. I was in Mexico City for the first time for some band stuff, and the gentlemen who were putting on the show were taking us around to be tourists. The three of them were very thoughtful and attentive, but they were for-real music nerds and therefore for-real nerds. As a nerd myself, I can make this determination with authority when presented with such fine specimens as them.

One of them had heard about a party and asked us if my bandmate and I wanted to go. This was a party that the head of Creation Records and the singer from the Libertines were DJing at, and it was in the richest part of the city. I couldn't give a fuck about that kind of thing, but the guys seemed jacked. They kept furiously whispering to each other that there was no way they could get us in, but one of them kept insisting the owner of the dirt club we were playing at owned the apartment that was hosting the party, and they could make it happen. It was cute and sweet to watch them white-knuckle debate the setting-up of a cool night.

The apartment was all glass and out of James Bond, but somehow they did indeed get us in. The party was on the roof and was fancy with a capital *F*. There was security with coiled-wire earpieces, free booze, big plants in planters, a million pillows and puffy couches, and everything was clean and glowing in white. Diverting and kind of tedious, still 'twas like all parties. I was introduced to the Libertines guy. He was friendly. There was a gym on the bottom floor that you could see from the elevator. I asked him if he wanted a piggyback ride while I ran on the treadmill. He thought this was a great idea, climbed on my back, and we headed down. Do you like good music, sweet soul music?

He was wearing a classic motorcycle jacket and, as drunk as he was, smelled expensive. As the elevator was closing, we could hear the security freaking out, so when we got to the bottom, we blocked the door with a trash can so it wouldn't close and couldn't go back up. We got on the treadmill and he put his head on my shoulder as I bopped along in fitness, wearing the lush's backpack.

The gym was at the bottom of the glassed-in breezeway, and we could watch the tumble as the security guards ran down the stairs to come and get us. They looked like the very concerned parent robots of spoiled-child robots. We were laughing when they arrived, and they super politely and, with "Guys, please, you're going to get us fired" expressions, put their cutting board-sized hands gently on our backs as they led us back up.

My bandmate could not get the dance floor started, so she began to take all the pillows that were on the ground and all the cushions off the couches to make a giant, abstract fort. She demanded that people sitting on the couches get up and give her the cushions. To their credit, the people there thought it was funny, so they did it.

She'd started her smushy construction as soon as the security guys left to stop our insane pig ride, so she had a pretty decent head start by the time we got back. They were still winded and distracted from running down the stairs, so they didn't notice at first. Right away, I started to help her build, and the fort grew and grew and grew . . .

After an amusingly long time, the guards snapped back to reality and saw what we were doing. They mistakenly believed we were among the honored and British guests, so they flapped and circled around us, unable to decide how to act. There was a frenzy of radio chatter between them and the Boss of No Fun. He decreed that they should very carefully start to disassemble the forts and turn them back into couches but not confront or even talk to us. There were only two of us and about ten of them, so they could take things apart much faster than we could build them. We knew we were pushing our luck so we didn't argue, but neither did we stop building until they were done unbuilding.

Sitting near the edge of the roof was a group of four or five women. One of them was looking at me and, maneuvered by a dream, I walked over and started to talk. Perhaps the confidence of having imposed glerk-glonk trouble on the night without consequence made me think I could keep it up. She said her name was Daniella. She had long brown hair and a vulnerable face. She was smart, spoke English well enough that I didn't have to embarrass myself too much with Spanish, and had a bewitching laugh. Her nose looked as if it had been broken a long time ago and was crooked in a nice way. I had broken my nose, too, and I told her hers looked cool. She told me she hated it and that I should shut up.

The guys who took us there said we were invited to a different party given by the son of a famous art collector in an even more ridiculous apartment. I asked Daniella and her friends if they wanted to come, too, and our music-nerd hosts were too nervous to deny them or us. Normally, even if I'd been distilled to my essential spirits, I would not have had it in me to keep this self-possession ruse up, but, geography nudging things along, the Centzon Tōtōchtin were with me.

Our next destination was close by; we walked a couple dazzling blocks and went up a dazzling elevator and through a dazzling penthouse double door. The party was small and the person who invited us seemed preoccupied with a number of just-underage male sex workers. He said hello by twirling his finger in the air without looking at us. I stood by the wall, stupefied by the original art deco everything, and talked to Daniella. She was charming, and this helped me to feel a little charming. We heisted booze from expensive frosted bottles, trying to catch the eye of the host to see if this was OK. He was busy nuzzling his way through the arms of several boyhoods and was too rich to care.

The one and only move I have is to be direct. If people aren't into it, they can't get grossed out with Nitwit Casanova because he never shows up, and its being brief makes it easy to shrug off if things go badly.

"Do you want to go into the bathroom and mess around?"

"What is 'mess around'?"

"Make out."

"Hahahaha, are you a teenager?"

I laughed too and let it go.

We kept talking about zoo animals and museums, and then she said, "Do you still want to mess about?"

The bathroom had no lock and people kept coming in, but we tried. She closed her eyes and asked me if I wanted to go home with her. I hadn't had real sex in eighteen months. After Lois and my trapped-as-depressing-roommates, mutual-dating moratorium, and after I'd moved back to Oakland, even though I was dying for it and because I was so plainly dying for it, I met no one. Most of my time was spent at home alone or drinking alone at a bar reading, and no one looks like a bigger creep than someone making the ostentatious point of being *alone*.

My first thought was that I would cum too fast, and my second thought had something to do with disbelief. Climbing through my jumbled face, she whispered, "Did I say something wrong?"

I told the head music-nerd guy I was leaving with her, and he looked at me like he'd won a medal. We got into a cab and she put her head on my shoulder.

Like a lot of unmarried grown-ups in Mexico, she lived with her parents. The apartment had a puzzling but educated person's layout. There were several large, covered birdcages in the courtyard. We went right to her room. It was dark, and I only remember there being cream-colored sheets and cream-colored pillows. She took off her clothes, and then she took off my clothes. Her body was preposterous—maybe the best body I have seen on a real person. Mine is not at all like that, so bummer for her.

142

I tried to go down on her, but she grabbed my ears and pulled me up hard. I told her I liked doing it, but she just looked uncomfortable. The rest was nice, though, I think. She seemed turned on and sensual, and I didn't cum too fast for being so out of practice. I was fucking her from behind and lightly spanked her on the ass; she looked over her shoulder and had a slightly anime-cowering but also a scolding, "C'mon, dude" expression. She was thirty years old, but it seemed like some things hadn't come her way yet. I couldn't decide if this blotched or heightened her beauty. She had a sturdy tongue.

The next morning, I had to be at an unnecessary-feeling interview pretty early. She said she would drive me. We were both hungover but grinning and without regrets. On the way to her sensible car, we were stopped by one of the world's many feculent cops. She told me not to say anything. The two of them stepped away a few feet and she handed him some money. He never looked at her while they were talking and stuffed the bills in his underwear waistband. Before we were in the car, he was fucking with someone else. She was annoyed but not at all undone by this and said it happened all the fatuous time. She told me that it could get really bad for you if you argued, and stared at the windshield for a minute. Then she shouted, "Stab it and steer!" quoting *Wild at Heart*.

That night, we played our little show and it was fine. I made a bunch of mistakes, but no one seemed to mind except me. Afterward, she came to stay at the hotel we were put up in, but I was sharing the room with my bandmate. The room was long, longer than one would anticipate, and narrow. There were eight beds in a row with only about a foot between them and the wall to move through. Inside it was painted light purple and all the bed frames were a different pastel color, each with a nightstand painted in a slightly-different-but-similar shade to their corresponding bed frames. The light bulbs were yellow, making the unmatched colors match even worse. I've stayed in twenty thousand hotels and this one was, without a remote contender, the most seasick.

While my bandmate was in the shower, we banged out a hot and quick one with her on top. We pretended we hadn't been doing anything when we heard the water turn off. It's the only time I've ever cum with someone on top; I pulled out and shot on her holy behind. Before we went to sleep, we said that we both wanted "very much" to stay in touch.

We wrote a few letters and talked on the phone once or twice. She said she wanted to come visit me in Oakland but was foggy about the date. Not long after, I was in Torino working on a record and left her messages asking her flat-out three times when she wanted to come over, but she never replied. It began to feel like she'd changed her mind. Being in a beautiful city made it hurt a little more and a little less. At dinner with the musicians we were collaborating with, I banged my wineglass on the table to emphasize a point about lovelessness and the stem snapped into pieces. One of them said, "It seems you are correct." I put a not-entirely-unsharp piece of this glass into my wallet.

When I got home, I went on with the rest of my life, assuming I would never see her again. After a couple of weeks, she called and said she would be there in a week and would be staying for nine days. This seemed rash; nine days was a really long time to spend with a person I barely knew.

I tried to convince her that maybe just a three-day weekend might be a better idea, but she didn't feel the same way, and I didn't want to hurt her feelings by insisting.

Overwhelmed by waves of uncertainty until she arrived, I spent all the livelong day cleaning my apartment and going to the 24 Hour Fitness. I did not work on music at all. After all this cleaning, things looked not a lot different than they had before, but the scrubbing gave me something to do other than spin around.

At the airport, she snuck up on me and affectionately bumped the top of her head under my chin. She was shorter than I remembered, which made me hot. We drove in traffic back to my place. On the way there, I told her about all the things I had planned for the nine days. I didn't know that she had been to the Bay Area before and she'd already done most of the tourist dope I was leaning on to take up time.

Before we arrived, I told her I had a huge cactus collection, thinking I did, but when she got there and looked at it, I realized there were really only about twelve or thirteen and in not-very-big pots. She didn't bust me for exaggerating, though, but I could tell she thought it was strange.

Making small talk wasn't going well, so, trying to get her into bed, I kept deciding that she must be tired, which she kept denying. I eventually told her that I was tired, which I wasn't, and asked her to take a nap with me. She was a little impatient with this childishness but did it anyway. Immediately after we were done banging, she took out a book and started reading, so I did too. I was hoping sex would break the tension. After both of us read for like an hour, she started kissing me and we bummed it again. It was like

145

I'd hoped it would be the first time I tried, and things finally relaxed. We went out to dinner and I set the alarm for late, mostly to eat up some time by sleeping in. During the night, she bled all over my sheets and was mortified. I really didn't care, but she made me promise to take her to a store so she could buy me new ones. I still have them.

The next few days was a lot of trying to find things to do during the day that she hadn't done already and then fucking a lot at night. She still didn't want me to go down on her and she wouldn't go down on me. Her pussy was compact and densely hairy but didn't seem gross or anything, so I couldn't figure out why she didn't want me to get in there. I asked a lot about what she was into, but she was shy talking about it, though she still wanted to do it at least twice a day. She said she wasn't used to sex lasting for so long, and it seemed like getting really thoroughly pounded cranked her up.

One night, after we went to a bar and came back a little tipsy, we started to fuck on the beanbag in my living room. She panted, "Come inside, come inside." I came inside her but became hard again right away and kept fucking her. I came another two times inside her without ever getting soft or pulling out. This had never happened before, and it never happened again.

She asked me if I'd finished but, knowing how shy she was to talk frankly about sex, I was unsure how to explain how unbreakably I had gushed my brains out over and over again into her remarkable and forbidden slit. I said, "Yes, I finished three times." She looked like she didn't totally believe this, which wasn't unreasonable, and got out from under me to lay on the rug. Her mind seemed to be working. As noted, she had an unbelievable body, but more and more I gathered she was still figuring out how to use it.

A few more days passed, and although she was incredibly pleasant, I could not be myself around her. She wasn't a total square but was certainly and genuinely sweet. I found I was pretending to be softer, less exposed, and less inclined toward the shadow realm than I really am. Basically, she was a truly nice, truly smart, and pretty normal woman, and I would never know what to do to make her happy. She wanted to leave movies that were too violent and wanted to leave art shows that were too disturbing. We kept fucking without any variation every day, but she seemed to like it more and more; she started talking more and more and laughing more and more.

On the day before she was going back, we drove to a nature preserve to go bird-watching. She intimated that the silence and waiting for birds were dull but was courteous about it; it *is*, in fact, dull, and that is part of the appeal. We watched an enormous raccoon swimming in a pond after some ducks. The raccoon was working so hard to catch them, but the ducks just quacked and easily paddled a few feet out of its way.

We went to dinner and I told her I was going to wash my hands, but I stayed in the bathroom for twenty minutes, playing chess on my phone. She thought it was funny when I spoke Spanish like a Mexican radio announcer, so I did that the whole drive home. Daniella had a red-eye flight that morning, and I told her I had work to catch up on and was going to go to an internet café to do it but said I needed to be alone to concentrate. When I got back, she was wearing a slip and sitting on my balcony, reading a book and biting her nails. I wanted to die.

I thought maybe it could work if she were more of a degenerate, so I asked her if she wanted to fuck my ass with a strap-on. She took several deep breaths, and for a moment I was frightened she did not know what I was talking about and I had embarrassed her. Then she whispered, "Please let me."

I went to the bathroom to wash my ass out and when I came back, she had gotten completely dressed in khaki pants and a flower-printed blouse. I figured she had changed her mind, but she took me by the hand and led me onto the bed. It wasn't really a bed, just a futon roll with a foam pad. She wrapped her arms around me and said, "Be tender first." We hugged deeply, and I wondered what was going through her mind, how faraway from home this seemed to her, if at all. She squeezed me long and tight, as though she were counting to thirty to reassure herself. The pressure in the room bent the glass in the windowpanes.

I had bought the harness and tiny red dildo we were going to use a few years ago for someone else. Love left the alpine village, though, and never came back. The dildo had never been used; it was pure and, for now, just hers. She kept her clothes on and was shaking, so I didn't want to suggest she be naked. I put the gear on over her pants and leaned against the wall, ass arched. I took her hand and stuck her finger up me. Her shaking was so intense, I could feel it all through my body. Her unbearably perfect breasts were heaving in a classic romance-novel way. This touched my heart and filled it with dread.

When she inserted the toy in me, she moaned a low creature's moan. She pumped at it with excessive care and grunted and succumbed. It felt like for her the walls were beginning to bend along with the windows. I wanted so much to feel happy for her, but I didn't feel anything other than nothing. Somewhere, I knew before even suggesting anything to her that my wanting to change her to be who she was not and my wanting to change myself to not be terrified that she was willing to make this effort would, in absolute certainty, lead to nowhere.

I didn't want to get any shit or lube on her clothes, so I unclasped the dildo and kept it in me like a stopper as I hobbled to the bathroom. When I got back, she was still dressed and had gotten so wet it left a big spot through her pants. I would have crawled all over anyone else that this might have happened to, but I could only put my cheek against hers in the dark. It was impossible to accept that Daniella wanted this or me.

She looked at my cock and asked me to put it in her mouth. She let it in about half an inch and did not move it, just held it in place. Her eyes were clamped tight in this moment for herself. Then I drove her to the airport.

When we arrived, Daniella touched my lips and said to me as I got out her suitcase from the car, "You know I love you."

At my one second of quiet, her eyes filled with tears. She straightened her back and ran toward the glass doors. She tripped before getting inside and a security guard helped her up. I was so glad she didn't turn around to confirm that I saw this, but I am sure she knew I did. I felt as if I had been set free from having been stuffed under a sink, and I was disgusted with myself. Earlier in the week, we'd gone to Moe's Books and I'd bought volume two of the *Russian Criminal Tattoo Encyclopaedia*. I went home and drank into and past the void, looking through the merciless renderings of the book and waiting for the sun to come up.

Daniella called me really late at night, four months later. She was so wasted, it was hard to understand what she was saying. I could make out that she wanted me to love her and asked what was wrong with her. I did my best to assure her that she was well rid of me, knowing that the white dwarf we'd already had was as much as I would ever have been able to give her.

In the Russian tattoo book, there's an illustration of a crying woman with dark hair wearing handcuffs with her palms placed against the sides of her face. I got it on my arm and I wanted to frame the part of the bedsheet Daniella had bled on, but she'd washed them, and the blood was gone.

AHMED KHOURY

An old friend from when I worked for five minutes in a hot-sauce factory, Kory, moved from Gilroy to Berkeley and asked if I wanted to get a drink. We bought some appalling malt liquor and sat at a bus stop near the immense entrance of a cemetery. The bus bench was under a tree and there was no streetlight, so we could see out from the shadows but no one could see us. We watched the sorrow's child people at the outdoor bar across the street look around while we made funny noises in the dark.

After a bit, I approached the locked cemetery gate and Kory told me to climb over it. I put my hand on it and was zapped by the primordial scary monsters on the other side. My body refused to move forward, and I was squealing and frozen by the hilarious electric current of the ghosts.

We were getting further buzzed, and Kory told me his cousin was around and wanted to get laid. He knew I was sad and on the make.

"What's your cousin's name?"

"Ahmed Khoury."

"Wait, so if he was your brother, your name would be Kory Khoury?"

"Har har fucking HAT!" he yelled, now drunk.

Ahmed and I met at a piano bar in Oakland that's been around since the 1930s. The singer, ye olde Rod Dibble, RIP (Rest in Pianos), played there six nights a week. People sat next to him and would go around in a circle to duet. Some were frat morons and hammed it up; some were disarmingly serious and brought their own saxophones or maracas to play along. I knew the night would be OK when Ahmed asked that we not sit right at the piano.

"Close enough to watch but far enough away to be safe from having to participate," he said.

We talked and drank a few and then went back to my new apartment in Fruitvale. He was not very good in bed, but his body was hot. He was around my height but stronger than me and had a good face. His cock was the right size for my asshole, but he could not fuck it right to save his life. Even though I hadn't had any in a bit, I could've done without it. He was like a container of baking soda or a tired cow leaning against a fence. It was strange because when he was done, he became all snuggles. Usually, a person who's checked out jets afterward. It wasn't dreadful, but it was a letdown. I asked him if he wanted to watch me jerk it so I could finish, but he said he was good and just wanted to hug. I told myself that was nice, at least, as we hugged and hugged and hugged and hugged.

We never really went out again anywhere after that. He just came over a couple more times and we had the same one-sided sexyless sex and the same summer festival of embrace afterward. I didn't come all three times we got together, and he never put any effort into making it happen. In conversation he was attentive, very funny, and peculiar, but naked he was a beautiful but pointless asteroid. I started the fade-out. This was not the coolest way to deal with him, but it wasn't the uncoolest, either, considering what an odd fuck he was.

Three months after we last talked, he was in front of my apartment, waiting for me. He seemed rational and calm and wanted to know why I had stopped calling him. It was neither rational nor calm to wait that long to ask this and then just show up, but I've done worse.

In a roundabout but sort of tipping-over way, I tried to explain that the sex was not working. He seemed deeply perplexed. Then I told him it wasn't working out because he was a lemon tree and I was the road to nowhere. I thought this would be funny, but he didn't like it. A week later, I found him behind me in his car while I was riding my bike to the grocery store. This freaked me out, but some scampering instinct told me to pretend I hadn't noticed. From spy movies, I remembered you could observe people following you using, in this case, the reflections of the freezer-aisle doors and the angled shoplifting mirrors above the pharmacy. His usual style was muted and tasteful, but on this day he was wearing orange raver pants, mismatched neon running shoes, and a satin crew jacket from *The Sopranos*. To keep from blowing up and confronting him, I tried to believe him being here might have been a coincidence, but then our eyes met in one of the high mirrors. Apparently, he had seen the same movies. In the glass, I made the aggressive universal gesture for *What?!* He turned around and left, and I never saw him again.

A year later, I got a call at 11 p.m. An older woman whose voice I didn't recognize was wailing on the other end of the phone. It's easy for me to accept and gloss over the insanity of people I do not love and to compartmentalize my place in and my role or lack of a role in that insanity. Maybe after having dealt with so much crazy, I'm able to be logical about illogic. Maybe after having dealt with so much crazy, I just say, "Fuck you, crazy. Get out of my fucking face. I hate your fucking guts," and then forget about it.

"My little baby chopped up his own face and pulled the skin off with pliers! Now he's dead! He is dead! He cut off his face because of you! You're the reason!"

"Uh . . . Jesus Christ! Jesus Christ! I'm sorry, I'm sorry—who is this?"

"AHHHHHHH! This is Ahmed's mother! This is Mrs. Khoury! Die, die, die! I want you to die!" There was panting quiet on the phone for a minute, and then she hung up.

ALBERT VU

I love to eat too much and I love to drink too much, but I'm also super vain, so I go to the gym a lot. I would probably be in phenomenal shape if all my effort wasn't just to blot out last night's gluttony. Exercising is a drag, so I check out the hot people to make time go faster. More or less, I am too introverted to do anything about it, and it is socially unclear if it's acceptable to hit on people while they're working out anyway. I have kilograms and kilograms of gym crushes to whom I have never even waved. Even though I've seen these certain people in the same humidor five days a week for years, I kid myself and I pretend to wonder if they like my shy little glances when I walk by. The Horde of Indifference I am met with make it clear that they have no opinion at all of the finky little wimp casually touching his toes almost near them. But—although only twice in more than a decade and half of double-negative squattings and curlings—I have at least *been* approached twice.

The first person was at the notoriously soiled and duct-taped 24 Hour Fitness in Koreatown, Los Angeles. A woman I never remembered seeing before walked right up to me and scatteringly did something I myself could never have been brave enough to do: "Hi . . . I know we don't know each other . . . but I, uh, have seen you coming here for a long time . . . "

Her teeth were meth teeth, her hair was maybe falling out, she was improperly thin, and her fingers were heavily bandaged. People who have crossed the threshold into the decline of Western civilization normally don't rattle me that much, but with her, I was alarmed and extra awkwardly frozen. With psychotic formality, I shook her hand too firmly, stentoriously asked her name, and then turned around and walked off. She seemed confused because what I did was confusing, and she followed after me trying to talk some more in a normal way. I looked over my shoulder and said, "No, nope, nope, no," and then she stopped following me.

She was wearing a white FUBU sweatsuit and in one of the mirrors, I saw it blur into the nighttime out and through the glass exit doors. Hand-wringingly, I told my friend about what had happened and what I'd done, and she said she was tired of listening to me overthink my "innate shittiness." All seventy volumes of the *Encyclopedia of Gremlins, Imps, and Trolls* slapped hard across my throat and chin . . .

Albert was short and very muscular. He and I passed each other in the weight room on some weekdays. His face was a miracle, and his pickup line was like a coppersmith's mallet: "You have a nice body—what's your number?" His voice was slow and clear. It was the first time anyone had ever told me I had a nice body. I was and am so wigged out about how peculiar and uneven my body looks that it's only by the entirety of the spirit world having sewed my mouth shut that I didn't barf this, my mirror's misgivings, to him right then and there.

Albert called me and the conversation was a dumb block of cement sitting in front of an anxious block of cement. I suggested the movies so we wouldn't have to talk, which would have been impossible anyway. I was trying to figure out how to deal with having pretty gnarly depression a little better, and to keep my rotting brain from sliding away, I started to be super rigid about my schedule. This is something that's proved to be an absolute must for me to get through life intact. The necessary regimentation has become so necessarily regimented that, without shame or dignified pause, I use colored pencils to draw up a chart twice a month. The day he asked if we could go out was a day I always went to the gym. I told him that we could meet in the parking lot after I was done.

He showed up wearing shiny gray dress pants and a tight purple shirt with a tie. His muscles looked real good. I think because I thought he was a dodo, I felt like I could be controlling; I didn't change out of my gym clothes but put on a heavy, long, brown 1950s cashmere overcoat I bought at Aardvark's in the eleventh grade. A seagull had shit on the lapel the first day I wore it to school. He looked at me and seemed disappointed that I was dressed so stupidly, and I didn't blame him.

We got into his car and he said he was hungry and wanted to get Italian food. We went into the first place we drove past. It didn't look very nice inside but he didn't seem to notice. He smiled and I smiled. The pasta he ordered was something like triple garlic and nothing else. I wanted to kiss him and now I was worried. He ate half of it while looking at bike racing on the loud TV and we tried to talk about the riders. The waiter boxed up the other half of Albert's food for him, and when we left he put it on his lap as he drove and kept eating it.

The movie theater was in a suburb I had never heard of. It seemed cleaner and richer than the rest of the city. I was embarrassed he was trying to impress me and then embarrassed I assumed he was trying to impress me. He chose a romantic comedy that no one would ever want to see in ten million years, and then I was afraid he was trying to be romantic too. The theater was enormous and there were only a few other people there, all of them couples and all of them looking as out of place in their shoddiness as I did.

As soon as the previews were over, he leaned over in his seat and pulled down my gym pants. I was still wearing my big coat. He started to suck me, and I ran my hand all over his impressive back. It felt commendable, and he did me for a long time, which made the movie less boring because romantic comedies are less boring if your dick is in someone's mouth. He was mostly a pro at sucking, but I could feel the garlic oil and food in his mouth a little.

He came up, never looked at me or kissed me, and immediately absorbed himself into the screen. I looked down and he was rubbing himself. Because of the giant overcoat, it was too difficult for me to lean over, too, so I got down on my knees on the ground and took a look in the flickering light. His cock was just like him, short and thick and pretty. It looked like if you squeezed it, a little scroll with the word *D'uh* printed on it would pop out of the urethra. I blew him, and he pushed my head down hard. He was not very long and I could easily get him all the way in. I tucked my lips around my teeth and self-consciously tried to make as much spit as

I could. He jacked my head up and down and, just before he was going to cum, pulled me up by the hair and pushed his fingers hard on his perineum so he wouldn't shoot, his eyes remaining on the screen.

When the movie ended, Albert surprised me by holding my hand as we walked out. I was quite sure we would not be going out again, but thankfully I did not yank my hand away. My internal snobbish dismissal of him would have been too much for me to bear if I'd made it physically obvious. He silently drove me back to my car in the gym parking lot and when I got out, I walked around to his driver's side door and motioned for him to roll down the window. Then I pulled down my pants and shoved my cock into the car and into his face. He smiled, took it in his mouth for a few seconds, then started laughing and drove away waving. I felt pretty good about myself for ending an undistinguished date with a sassy cherry on top.

I didn't see him the next week at the gym, which was not unusual; he wasn't as uptight as me about going at the exact same times. He called me and I kept cutting it short and being unsubtly busy when he wanted to meet again. His final few calls I did not pick up at all.

He worked out with a group of four other short, queer guys. They were all in good shape, but he was the king for sure. When I finally did see him at the gym, I walked by, trying to be cool, and said hi. He pointedly turned his back to me and all of his friends stared a hex, one of them baring his teeth.

Being too dense or I-don't-know-what, I would keep saying hi when I passed him and was always met with the same hostile cavity. There is no way I can explain why I didn't just stop. I don't think I was trying to be a meanie or trying to exert some dominance over him in the way that I had by not dressing up for our date. He was so hot and strong, maybe I was desperately hypnotized by his brute force, or maybe I got so little attention otherwise that even when I didn't want it to work out, I couldn't stop the senseless pressing and pressing. All seventy volumes of the *Encyclopedia of Wights, Hobgoblins, and Gymtrash* slapped hard across my ankle and wrist . . .

This went on for almost three months. I had become sickening. Finally, in the locker room, completely naked, one of the men in his crew grabbed my wrist, rapped his knuckle into my chest, and said, "Albert really liked you, but now nobody likes you. Fuck off or else."

There was no reason not to believe him.

MOIRA CARTER, NEW YORK

Sometimes I like New York and sometimes it makes me feel like shit. Probably everyone feels this way about New York. I was working there on an installation and concert based on—but also an erasure of—the opera *The Magic Flute*. It was at a gallery at NYU and I was staying in a visiting professor's apartment for a month. Everyone involved in the project was incredibly good and, in no small way, art idols of mine. But the winter was especially cold and Yuck York is lonely.

I posted on the internet:

Do you want or need a spanking? Do you live in NYC? If so, reply under subject heading SPANK SPANK. Serious only please. Neither Hope, nor Wonder, nor Despair.

One person wrote me.

Moira and I started to talk over email and it became clear really quickly that a miracle unmade of darkness had occurred. I asked her for a photo and asked her how old she was. What she sent showed a pretty, kind of punk-industrial Betty Page-looking woman in a sweater, with a hint of a smile. You could send it to your mom. Her lips were very full and almost fancifully made-up. Her face was healthy and rounded, and she had perfect hair. She said she liked that I checked on her age.

I explained the rules. She could accept them and it would work out, or she could not accept them and I would wish her well and adieu. I was going to call her "little moira" and she was going to call me MISTER. Anytime she would write to MISTER as little moira, she had to type IN ALL CAPS. If she needed to talk to me outside of little moira party for whatever functional reason, then the rule was to use regular type but put it in parentheses. I told her that if I gave her an order, she had to complete it within the stated amount of time or the game was over. If she didn't want to do something, we had to discuss it beforehand outside of the game but that there were no second chances once she said YES MISTER. Basically, I said, *I am going to give you dirty homework and you have to do your homework on time, no distant promises.* I said nothing would be too terrible and the regulations were to weed out any nondevotees. She said she loved it already.

The first thing she had to do was tell me why she deserved to be spanked. What were the bad things she had done? How hard did she want to be spanked? Then she had to send two photos in very specific poses. One was a side view, cheek against the wall, on her knees and grabbing her ass. The other one was facedown on a pillow. She had forty-eight hours to complete these or else. In about an hour, she wrote back and said she deserved to be spanked because she did not believe in her own ambition nor did she finish her projects. She wrote "this is how hard I want to be spanked" and it was a picture of bruises the size of potatoes.

The other posed photos she sent back were exactly what I ordered. They were perfect, actually. Her body, which hadn't been clear from the first sweater portrait, made me gasp. She was in panties and no bra. Her thighs were like hams, her boobs were small but absurdly erect, and her ass was like a melon. Her fingers were dug so deeply into it I could not see the first joint. In the other, she'd smashed her face all the way into the pillow and I could see the strain in her neck muscles. *Oh fuck*, I thought.

She wrote and said she liked how I talked to her. She said I was mean but not too mean and that she wanted to come over. I wrote and said she was a good girl for doing what she was told and I wanted her to come over too. To play at being a halfway-OK person, I fumblingly tried to tell her to let someone know where I was staying so she wouldn't feel like she was going to get disappeared. She said she would leave bread crumbs all over to and from Queens, but was clearly uninterested and even a little annoyed at my paternalism. We set a date and I began to jack off rabidly every twenty minutes.

The only time she could meet was after midnight. I took a nap, woke up around 11 p.m., got cleaned, sent her a taxi voucher, and waited. She called and said she would be about forty-five minutes late. That was OK. We had a hard time finding each other after she was dropped off because the buildings in the area were numbered in an illogical way, but she eventually figured it out and was walking up the correct path. I waved her inside, out of the snow.

In the elevator, I tried to act formal and distant to keep up MISTER appearances. I pointed to the side of my forehead, not looking at her, and she knew to give it a kiss. Her face was a lot thinner than in her photos, like she-maybe-hadn't-been-eating-enough thinner. Her makeup foundation was not quite the right color and seemed to be clotting a little. But her hair looked astonishing, her nails were filed to points like almond daggers, and she wore the color and type of heels I told her to. She was looking at me out of the corner of her eye over the collar of her huge fake-fur coat—smirking, lupine, and ready.

When we got inside, which was several floors up, I asked her if she wanted a drink, which she declined. I told her that was the last solicitous thing I was going to do all night and she said, "Thank God."

Oh fuck, I thought.

I pointed to a couch and told her to get on her knees and face the window behind it. She skipped across the room to it. She pulled up her tight gray dress and I saw her geographic expanse of ass for the first time. It was wrapped in sheer, champagne-colored panties.

She'd seemed like a pro at this when we'd talked and although I had spanked a lot of people before, I wanted to make sure I really knew what I was doing for her, so I looked some things up and had read to alternate between making the number of smashes predictable but increasingly intense and then, at times, add a shock of very rough or very soft.

I hit her with my hand, eight on one ass, eight on the other, and got harder and harder. She started to breathe a little deeper and buck. I rubbed her marks and could feel the heat coming off before I touched her. There were a lot of academic journals and tourist coffee-table books all around the apartment. She pulled her panties down around her knees. I picked up a photo book about the construction of the Brooklyn Bridge and started to tap her with it and then swung like I was trying to crush a scorpion. She arched her back deeply, and her unthinkable thighs were visibly shaking. I asked her if she wanted it to continue or if she wanted to stop. She said she needed a break for a couple minutes but would want more. Then she said, "It can never be hard enough, and there is no way I can get enough."

She stayed facing the wall, and after a little bit, I took off my belt.

I've pulled this move a lot of times. It's a wide, black police belt. One was around my waist when I was born, and I have worn them ever since. . . . This night's was a little newer. I gave the previous one away to an incredibly deserving bad person two years before. It's kind of a cliché, but the sound of the dead leather swishing through pants belt loops is a certain and right tone for nights like this.

She started to take off more of her clothes and was now only wearing a bra and high heels. I doubled the belt in half to keep it from snapping her around the front, wrapped my arm around her hips, and with my belt-wound hand forced her legs apart. This was the first time I really touched her aside from spanking. She was as meaty as she was incredibly firm. The belt came down with our desired effect. She started getting louder and her ass skin was going from bright hot pink to having little flecks of red. I smoothed my hand all over it and hit her some more.

She panted, "Spank my Black ass. I want you to say, 'I am going to spank your Black ass.'"

To me, she looked like a white person. Being a state-college, middle-class, stone honky myself, this made me feel real weird. She was, although old enough, a lot younger than me, and I thought, *Maybe people her age are less uptight about race than people my age?* Also, she was going pretty full-on doing what I wanted to do and I wanted to be game, so I feebly muttered it a couple times under my breath.

My arm was getting tired. I needed to rest, so I got her a glass of water and then stood behind her to look at what we had done. Her eyes were closed and she moved over to press her face against the cold window, fogging and fogging it.

Her pussy, I could see now, was like a pinhole camera for which no civil nor spiritual toll could have prepared me. It seemed so small, like a smooth, rose-colored collectible toy. I mentioned this to her and she agreed, "Yes, it is very small." I asked her if she wanted me to touch it and she said, "A lot."

I ran my finger over it in awe, and then I put on a cock ring and a rubber, and we started to fuck.

It was difficult to fit inside of her. She was wet but still needed a lot of lube. We moved to the bed and kissed and fucked more. I had to pump very slowly and she had to stop every few minutes. Then I would lick her out and then fuck for a couple minutes and then lick her out more. When she needed to stop, she would say, "OK, OK, OK," I would pull out, and we would do other things. When we kissed, her mouth was a cushion. It went on like this—fucking for a few minutes and then stopping. It was hard to tell if her having such a tight hole was amazing or a drag. I asked her if she still liked it and she said yes but that it got to be too much because she was just a little speck of dust.

She gave me kind-of-whatever-but-enthusiastic head; however, she performed the most outstanding hand job I have ever received. As soon as she wrapped her hand around my cock, the cathedral dome of earth toppled to the sand and all

I could do was hilariously say, "Wow." She did not really do much as far as jacking, but it was something about her grip, the snug and soft texture of her palm, and how her dangerous fingernails looked around me. I told her she was a genius at this and she said other people had told her so too.

We had been chopping down the forest for about three hours. If her ass could take more, her pussy couldn't, and from all the smashing, neither could my arm. The bedroom in that apartment had two twin beds. She lay in sweat on one and I lay in sweat on the other. We started to talk and get to know each other a little.

She told me she was a comedian and that her father was Black and from Trinidad. She said Black people could tell she was mixed but most white people couldn't. I'd never hung out with someone in comedy before and asked her a lot of questions. Some things were the same as music-business barbarisms, and some weren't. She told me about famous comics she knew that were maniacal assholes and which ones she had "balled." I noticed she had a tattoo of the symbol for the band I play in in on her forearm, but I didn't mention it, and she didn't either. It came out that I'd written some music for a play that her best friend and roommate did and that he would be dankly amused, though would outwardly feign mortification if he knew what we had been doing. She was funny and nice. In some ways, her thoughts on existence were annoyingly younger than I would have expected—more seventeen than twenty-five—but she was appealing in a lot of ways and didn't seem problematically crazy.

At 5 a.m., she got dressed and I called her a car. On the way down in the elevator, she said, "You are kind of normal."

I couldn't tell if she was making fun of me. I made an exces-sively wide sweep of telling her that I generally wasn't really into talking much, and she snickeringly looked at me like this went without saying.

After thirty-six hours, I started to write her every day, and we set up another date. I asked her how she was and she said that her cunt felt like a truck drove through it because of the cheap garbage lube I had. She wanted to do it again soon, though.

Between seeing each other again, there was the shoot-ing in San Bernardino at the Department of Public Health, which was a short and straight line east of my apartment at home. It hit me harder than other shootings. Dispirited, I talked to my mom about it and she told me to remember that most people are trying every day to be good, and the only plausible reaction is to put one's entire heart into whatever you're doing. A lot of times, I feel like working on music is futile, vain, and a waste of life, but this reminded me—at least that day—that it doesn't hurt anyone, that it tries to be something decent. At the opera rehearsal, I talked to the orchestra and choir about this idea. Their playing had been flabby and overconfident and every session, I had to lug them up a hill. To their credit, they committed and were excellent. Everyone forgot it the following day, but for a moment we were in it together.

As little moira and MISTER were preparing for their next date, I asked her if she was into anal and double penetration. She said yes to anal but that because she was so tight, DP might technically be too difficult. She said she would bring a small dildo and try it. She said knowingly that I seemed really into this. I told her I had only done it a couple times before in threesomes or with toys and that it was rad.

She showed up very late at night and proceeded to get beaten. This time, she lay across my lap. She weighed a lot, which I liked. Her body was substantial and could take a punch. I told her this, and she looked admiringly at herself in the reflection of my awe. I knew I could hit her harder this time and she liked it. We took more breaks because of this and there were slight-then-growing contusions and little-then-not-little cuts. It was her goal; she said she wanted it to be hard to walk.

When we got worked up from the pounding, I gave her head for a while. She said she never came with another person but that I could do it as long as I wanted. She tasted fresh. When it was time to fuck, she got out some better lube. It came in an aluminum tube and was called Uberlube. I told her I'd had a vasectomy and was clean, and I asked her if she had anything I needed to worry about. She said no and whimpered that she had never had anyone cum inside her and that she wanted me to. I put it in her ass with heroic ease on her part and she tried to fit the dildo in her pussy, but it was too much. I washed it and then we went at a normal bang. The lube made getting into her much easier, and even though we had to go pretty slow, I could tell she was getting more out of it. This time, I really felt her tightness and it was nonsensically good. It was like a stick of butter smashed between a hardcover copy of the biography of Marquis de Sade and a hardcover copy of the biography of Yukio Mishima.

Each time I was about to blow, I would pull out to hold it in. I watched her watch the tears of pre-cum. I told her to

169

squeeze my balls and she tried, but her vise was like a sleepy cricket's. She told me she was too weak. I asked her to really squeeze them as hard as she could; she tried, but she was, in fact, quite weak.

Her nipples were dead center and were pink. They felt firm, like the rest of her. They were both pierced, but she said the left one was infected and to only touch or suck the right one. Frenzied and all, I kept having to check which was which. I asked her how long it had been infected and she said almost a year. This struck me as something that one would have wanted to take care of, but they weren't my boobs, so who was I to judge.

It started getting deep and hot and I shot inside her. When I was out, she jammed her fingers way up her slit, dug out the jizz, and, looking me in the eye, ate it all up off her hand. This was a genuinely impressive maneuver. I thought about clapping, but I didn't want to dim the shine of her accomplishment by being goofy.

The shows I came to New York for finished, and during the after party, I spanked one of the curators, Marianne, and the dramaturge, Arthur, in the bathroom. Then the student part of the cast and some of the choir spanked me when I climbed up drunk onto one of the sets. I also spray-painted my chest and thighs with black lines in the gallery director's office. He started laughing and took some Polaroids. It was a saturated week.

When I got back to LA, Moira and I kept talking over text. When I went to the desert to celebrate cacti, she told me how much she wanted someone to murder her with a knife and leave her body in the sand for vultures and ravens to eat.

Christmas was coming, so I rode my bike to the hardware store and bought her two hammers with plastic yellow handles. When she received them in the mail, she sent me a photo of herself wearing red-black lipstick, holding one hammer against her temple and holding the other in her mouth. She said she was carrying them in both hands around her apartment to terrorize her roommate.

She asked me what I wanted for Christmas and I told her I wanted a video of her jerking it to climax and seven photos of her cleaning her room. There is a pretty tame but fun strip club in LA called Jumbo's Clown Room. It's never really that sexual for me; it's more to watch the dancers' far-out gymnastics. But once I was there and three of them came out with glass cleaner and paper towels to clean the body marks off the mirrored wall at the back of the stage. Beyond my control and without pride, this was the only time I've ever gotten hard at a strip club.

The order was sent by MISTER and accepted by little moira with a specific timeline and date. The video did not show up, so I thought she was playing and I started to berate her insolence. She wasn't replying, so I ramped up the game's tirade. After a while, she finally got back to me but was initially indirect about why she wasn't sending the video. Then she eventually said in parentheses that she just couldn't do it. It was the anniversary of a friend's suicide and she was too busted up. I said I was sorry and that I didn't realize what was going on.

A few days later, she sent the cleaning photos. Waiting in this game was against the regime, but she seemed so upset I didn't pretend to berate her. What I did finally get was just

OK. She only did four of the seven and these were clearly done halfheartedly; it looked like what she'd said about not completing things was true. It also felt like maybe I'd misread that she wanted a boss. She was clearly a masochist but maybe not really a sub. I guess I could have asked, and I guess she could have said. An unkind part of me wondered if her friend-dying meltdown was a way to get out of doing that video because it would have required some work and it would have required doing what she was told. It was the kind of lie that I would have told to get out of doing something I didn't feel like doing. Probably, though, I was just aggravated about death keeping me from getting what I wanted.

The next time we got together was in Philadelphia. The band I play in had a show in town and she took a direct bus there from New York. Rushing from the airport, I left a key for her at the desk of my hotel and then went to the venue. She would get there before I got back, so I also left my cop belt and cane in an X across the bed for her to find.

That night at the show, one of the other bands on the bill—a derivative, third-wave dilution of a riot grrrl band called Local Bruv—asked us about some lyrics they thought were racist as we were packing up. We played a song that questions racial fetishization: Is it OK to do it if someone likes it, is it ever acceptable, is it OK to like being fetishized, is it not always cool to be yourself, etc. I didn't think it was so hard to grasp that this was a song about questions, not declarations, and I was trying to wrap cables and get out of there, but they kept at me. I was exhausted from the flight and show and became agitated and I'm sure wasn't making myself even a little clear. They couldn't get beyond the chorus of the song being the phrase *Black dick* sung over and over. They had a song whose chorus was *Khmer Rouge!* over and over, so we pointed out that, following their logic, they must be pro-Khmer Rouge, but they just yelled at us more. I have a terrible, terrible, terrible habit of losing my temper, so I just yelled back even more loudly and crazily than they did. I became even less coherent and it devolved into a stupid, dumb, stupid, disgraceful mess that played out in public. It absolutely dismantled my mood and was largely my fault.

When I got back to the hotel, Moira was there and, I was happy to see, beaming at the X on the bed. I felt a little better after seeing her. I didn't go into detail about what happened but said people had given us shit about a song and that I'd handled it badly and needed a drink. I would be back in fifteen minutes. I ran through the street and found a yuppie bar. The drink helped, sort of. We went at it.

After mauling her ass with the belt and cane, the Goddess Fucky-Fuck happily arrived and abolished any remaining gloom. At one point, while sitting on Moira's back, I put the cane around her neck, but both of us realized there wasn't really a way to do this that wouldn't actually kill her. We laughed for a second and then laughed that we laughed at this.

She told me she wanted one million hickeys on her neck: visible, plum-sized, quietus-clip hickeys. Lying on top of her, cock inside, I tried my very best. At first, it was so hot I lost my mind and felt wonderfully and animally out of control. As with her ass, though, she could not be ravaged enough. After initially hanging upside down from the ceiling and then entering my spirit through a burrow at the base of my spine, a gargoyle rabbit wafted down to help by chomping and humping and sucking quite as hard and as monstrously—short of these efforts sending me to prison, as it could—but Moira demanded more and more. Eventually, its mouth surrendered in an admission to being fucked-out. With what little I had left, I bit down on her and pulled out to jerk cum onto her now-almost-equally-fucked-out cunt. She got up to survey in the mirror what I imagined must look like a genocide, but she just said, "Well, pretty good."

To try and make up for it, I started to whip her on the ass with the belt again. The person in the next room shouted, "No, no, no, enough, enough, enough! GOD! GOD!! GOD!!! STOP ALREADY!!!!" through the wall. I whipped her a few more times hard for good measure and then quit. I could see her thighs vibrating and I kissed and licked all over the cuts. We talked for about half an hour, and then she got dressed and left to stay at a friend's place.

With the day of traveling, playing a show, arguing at the show, and the senseless sex fiendishness, my heart, mind, and body were over. I had an early flight and turned on the TV to fall asleep. It wasn't on loud at all, but the person who'd shouted from next door threw what sounded like an end table against our shared wall. The lamps and paintings in the room clanked and shook and my head bounced on the pillow. I didn't turn the TV off, though.

As I was falling asleep, Moira called and said her friends were not waking up to let her in. Philadelphia has some rough neighborhoods and she felt worried. She apologized but asked if she could come back and sleep in my room. I have to wear earplugs and a sleep mask to fall asleep, and I grind my teeth, so I also have to wear a mouth guard: all holes filled. I told her I would be embarrassed by all this palliative gear, but of course, come back. I called her a car and let her in about thirty minutes later. I shook her hand as a joke when she arrived, and she climbed into the room's other bed. Even though I had to get up at 6:30 a.m., she was gone before I was awake. This was unexpected, and as I was taking a shower and getting ready to leave, I wondered what it would have been like to have woken up in the same room.

MOIRA CARTER,
LOS ANGELES

My birthday was coming, and I asked Moira if she would want to fly to LA if I bought her a plane ticket. I had a regular fuck buddy, for real and amazingly named Lana. I topped her, too, but she wasn't as into getting hit as Moira; she was more into being intensely used as a fuck toy and bossed around. I asked Lana if she wanted to play bad lieutenant and that I would order her to do bad-lieutenant things to Moira. She said yes and even bought Moira a thin, red sub's collar. Obviously, Moira said yes and obviously, I was really, really into this. It could only have been more perfect if, in the same room, there was an even-more-grown-up daddy to punish me for my own crimes on the highest rung of the dripping hierarchical ladder. But even as it lay, this was horribly close to being unfathomably hot.

Moira arrived as I was walking out the door to pick up Lana to drive her to the flop hotel I'd booked. My phone rang and it was Lana calling to say, through a yawn, that she'd changed her mind. Will-o'-the wisp but fantasy it proved to be! I told her it was irritating that she could not have figured this out at any time other than fifteen minutes before the date, but she and I are pals, so whatever. It was my birthday, so F-WORD being bummed!

When I got there, Moira seemed pointedly neutral regarding Lana not coming, which threw me off a little. She had also eaten a burrito right before and her breath was pretty grody. She had a nice mouth that would now have to be avoided. We did our thing. It was not as cuckoo or focused as usual but still fun. She gave me a velvet bag of magic-shop exploding rocks for my birthday. I told her thank you, that I liked practical gifts a lot, and we said good-night.

A taxi took me to The Varnish, which is my favorite bar. It used to be a speakeasy; the entrance is through a small door in the back of a famous restaurant downtown. I know this sounds super played-out and dangerously close to douchebaggery, but I still really like drinking there. They only let a set number of people in at a time so it's never too mobbed, it's dark, and they play 1960s soul or free jazz at a sane volume.

I sat, got out my Game Boy, and ordered a Red Ant, which is bourbon, mezcal, absinthe, and Cherry Heering; as one would imagine, it was witlessly strong. The server brought it over and I heard some regulars wish her a happy birthday. I told her it was my birthday, too, oafishly waving my driver's license as proof. She smiled and we highed a Piscean five. She gave me that drink on the house. After that, already blurrily losing at my video game, I ordered a bartender's choice. When she brought it over, she explained it was a rare tiki drink that had so much booze in it that whenever it was served, the policy was that whoever ordered it would be cut off for the rest of the night. She said everything was in it and, with a wink, said I should chug it. This was 1,000 percent up my alley. She put this one on the house, too, and was correct; it delightfully overturned my consciousness.

I left an absurdly huge mutual-birthday tip, bumped my face real hard on the coatrack, and rematerialized in front of two urinals. There was a plaque above each etched with the names of the famous people who had pissed here. During the pee, my head spun out and I loudly fell onto my ass. I was incapable of making any kind of decision and just sat there with my pants open, pretty wet with the remaining piss. A bounce man came in and pointed his thumb at the door. I said, "Good idea." He not-unsoftly hoisted me up by the arm and I went home.

Moira grew up in a little town in California, so she knew a lot of people in LA. A month later, she came for a visit. She was staying in a motel near MacArthur Park, which is a fascinating-but-not-real-safe part of the city. She looked especially hot when I showed up, and I could tell she had spent a long time getting ready.

For no good reason, I had started getting into porn where people pretended to be cats, so I brought a saucer and boxed water with me and ordered her to crawl across the room and lick up the water. When she got to the saucer, I would move it to the other side of the room. She sort of crawled back to it but gave me a less-than-inspired look, so I asked her if she was into this. She said she didn't like humiliation. I put my hands around her throat and she said that was better.

We had been together enough times that I was figuring out how to cram it into her in a way that felt better for both of us, but I felt a little embarrassed about the cat thing not working. After I whipped her ass to completion with a piece of bamboo and we were fucking, I tried to think of something that would make her like me again. I told her to say, "I want you to kill me." A huge smile broke out over her face.

As I fucked her, I squeezed her neck. She patted my hand to let go when it was enough, which for her meant until the blood vessels in her eyes burst. All the while, she was gasping and hissing as a chant, "I want you to kill me, I want you to kill me." It freaked me out and I left my body for a moment, but it was electric to see her seem satisfied. She kept the grin on her face when we were done and looked at the ceiling while I was getting dressed to leave.

She wrote me half an hour after I left, saying that some stocky, waffle-faced guys were hanging around at the motel and kept knocking on the door, asking her if she was a sex worker. I told her I thought this was maybe kinda funny? She said she thought so, too, kinda, but that she couldn't go outside. She wrote two hours later to say she had to call her friends to come get her because the guys still wouldn't leave. I should have come back and gotten her, but it wasn't what she would have wanted MISTER to have done.

Moira decided she was going to move to Los Angeles. She said it was because nothing was happening for her in comedy in New York and "for all the other reasons of why New York." She didn't have any job, any money, any creative plans, or anywhere set to live. She sublet or stayed with some friends of her parents or her own friends. Not having a place to be would have made me kill myself, and soon she didn't feel any differently. We would chat a little more casually now outside of little moiraville and carefully edged toward being quasi-regular chummy. When I tried to encourage her to work on art or said I would loan her a synth, her main vibe was *what's the point.* Helplessness, even in the face of pending despair, gets on my nerves, but considering our relationship, it wasn't my place to say anything. She was still into messing around, though.

I picked her up from a big 1930s apartment building in Koreatown and told her I was going to take her to the grand dame of bondage stores to buy her any whip she wanted as a welcome-to-Los-Angeles present. She knew about the store and said she looked at their catalog all the time. We caught up in the car and were both in good moods for our coming fuck plague.

The place did not disappoint, and she found an incredibly thick and wide black leather strap fixed to a handle. It was about three feet long and real heavy. In the car on the drive back, she gave it a little hug like it was a fuzzy kitten.

The lobby and stairwell of the building she was staying in had not been redecorated or restored since it was built. It looked cool, and it also looked haunted with down-on-their-luck bacteria. The apartment itself belonged to a goth friend of Moira's. It was caked with purple cat hair, it smelled like purple cat shit, and there were dirty purple dishes in the sink. With a broom and shovel, I tried to get the fireman's overalls of dander off and out of the futon. A month later, my WPA-sponsored infrastructure scrubbing was completed and I beat her ass to complete oblivion with the new strap. She was a really hot fuck that night. Moira took a razor and cut slits into her inner thighs, and when I went down on her, she crushed my face between her legs and I was covered with her blood. On the way back to my car, there was a ridiculous spring in my step.

We started to meet twice a month or so, with longer gaps in between when I was on tour. She did not seem to be having much success with jobs, art, or finding a decent place to stay. Every other time we got together, she was staying in a new place and seemed more insecure and uncertain about her life.

One was a USC student apartment that was packed with other people. She said we could fuck, but she couldn't get hit there because it made too much noise. The bed creaked very loudly, even when you sat on it. I guess the sounds of humping must have been OK, but she didn't want the other tenants to know what a pervert she was. I went there after I had gotten into a fight with a subhuman at my gym who was wearing a pro-AR-15 shirt the day after the Pulse nightclub shooting. I was shaken up, but Moira was gracious and understanding about it. I punched her in the arm really hard because it was quieter than spanking. This made her squeal and giggle, and later, she said that now her shoulder hurt all the time.

Another sublet had an old plaque on the stairs that said DELIVERIES IN REAR. I pointed this out to her and she flat-out guffawed and spread her cheeks apart. It was stupefying and I could not *not* fuck her up thee cinematic ass. This place was also crowded, and she said the women who lived there seemed to be crying all the time. On the wall there was a to-do note written by the person whose room she was subletting. It said, *Get Celexa, get Lexapro, get a towel, get white wine.*

We got together in this place three times. Each time, she seemed to be sadder and more withdrawn. I asked her if she still wanted to mess around and she said yes, but the wildness and ferocity was floating away from her. The last time we ever did it, there was an ugly feeling. She was, for the first time,

181

indisputably going through the motions. It felt like she was infirmly convincing herself that being beaten and fucked was an answer. I kept checking in, and she would just mumble that it was fine. As soon as we were done, she rolled to the side and was blank and off.

I told her it wouldn't be awful for us to talk for real if she wanted. She told me the actual reason that she'd left New York was that she had been beaten up by her last boyfriend at a party. She told me he threw her onto the bathroom floor and repeatedly stomped on her shins and chest while he poured shampoo into her eyes. People she considered her friends saw it happening, but no one helped her. Her mind was catching up with the horror this had left in her body.

We had done awful and wonderful things to each other, but we were not close enough for me to be completely there for her through something that important. I definitely couldn't hit, choke, and mark her up anymore, and I'd been wrong when I said we could talk for real. We did not love each other, and I was not her boyfriend. I unkindly figured I shouldn't call her until she called me, and she did not call me.

A couple months passed before I wrote to say hello. She was very angry that I hadn't gotten ahold of her. I told her she hadn't gotten ahold of me, either, which she brushed off. She asked me why. The deep-down real answer of me being afraid of her pain, not being invested enough in her, and being afraid of becoming that invested in her would have torn her to bits. I was well aware of how much a true friend would need to be there for her as she began to realize the trauma and implications of having been assaulted in such an especially horrifying way, and I was unwilling to be that true friend.

So I lied that Lana and I had started getting more serious. I told her that Lana was too threatened by her and had said that our physical misadventures were more than she could manage.

Moira insisted that I come to her new apartment and pick up some stuff I'd given her. I really didn't want to, but she wouldn't let it go. When I got there, it was hard times. The place had a huge hole in the ceiling, smelled distinctly unhappy, and, in the foyer, there was a cluttered and mixed-up donkey vainly trying to drag its upturned cart. Held in place with a Pacific Gas and Electric magnet on the refrigerator was a drawing I'd given her of carrots with eyes and mouths holding axes and swords. The living room had a pile of dirty clothes in the corner but no furniture. I told her she could use the space for performance art. We sat on her bed. I tried to lie again about everything, and she said she wanted to see me cry. We talked for about half an hour and I left all the stuff she wanted me to take, pretending I forgot it.

She was still mad, but neither of us had many friends to lose, so we started to hang out again a bit, though we weren't fucking or clobbering. We went to that bar I like, got severely wasted, and ended up at a twenty-four-hour diner in Little Tokyo. I took her to a museum music thing and ran into a friend of Lana's who was jealous of her, and she looked Moira up and down for what seemed like a full minute, then snickered theatrically. We got high and went to see a couple psychedelic movies at the New Beverly. Two of

Moira's toes were fused together and I'm really into physical discrepancies, so she would send me photos of them held up against screenshots of Salma Hayek. She asked me to make a recording of my sneezes, but I never did it.

She liked gyms as a fetish. She lived near the one I went to and would walk by it a lot. I took her inside to look around at the machines and pointed out which people were unhoused and lived there. It had lockers and showers, was safe, and membership was seventeen dollars a month. A smart move if you needed it, and the staff was tolerant. After making our circuit of caved-in social and economic promises, I suggested she slowly and with comic sensuality eat a huge, majestically unhealthy ice cream cone next to the front door. People about to or finishing their exercise were entering and exiting and could not avoid watching her eat it. We both thought it was densely funny; it was a sweet moment between us. She had taken to wearing a cock ring I'd left at her place by accident around her wrist as a bracelet.

Then I started to be on tour for months and we didn't see each other. Our communication dimmed in a natural way. When I was home for a short break, I asked what she was up to. She replied that she was working at a bubble tea shop, taking special effects makeup classes, and not getting fucked. She said she was only eating ramen and cheese and putting on weight. She sent some dirty pics and was carrying this weight very, very well.

I missed horrible things and asked if she felt together enough to try it again. She paused and said maybe, but no penetration. The pause made me feel like she wasn't ready, and I didn't want to open what wasn't my business to open.

It was too anguished and delicate to return to, hogs not fully and confidently loose.

I got more and more busy with music BS again, and again we talked a lot less. Every once in a while, one or the other of us would make a sexual overture, but one or the other of us would back off at the last minute. We made plans for me to come over and to bite and hickey up her ass. She said her room smelled like cat piss.

A lot had changed for me regarding my fear of drugs a few years prior. After taking MDMA as my maiden voyage at a friend's well-appointed New Year's Eve party, I, an inch at a time, began a deep and oceanic but cautious and positive relationship with ketamine, hippie-style hallucinogens, and marijuana. Being a grown-up at this point and, I guess, fairly responsible, they were doing me a lot of good as far as encouraging my heart to keep pressing on through our shitty world.

I was doing mushrooms that day and said I would be over when I returned to earth. She thought I was blowing her off, which I was not. I told her I was coming for sure and that I was very much looking forward to a daytime of ungovernable hypnotization alone and a nighttime of undomesticated corruption together. Moira called me a liar and was intensely hostile in a way she'd never been.

This, enforced by the cat piss, turned me off, and I didn't want to go over anymore. To divert but not omit having plans, I asked her if she wanted to see a movie with me in a few hours. She said yes, but when I was done being high and left to pick her up, she said she wouldn't be ready in time. It always took her about nine hundred hours to get ready. I said OK but that I was still going to the movie and would talk to her after. She was pissed I wasn't coming over, and I was annoyed she wasn't ready and bailed. That night, she started to criticize me and turned every word I said around in a way that, to me, did not make sense. *Fuck this*, I thought, *she's either become a dick or is going nuts.*

When we talked at all, it became more fraught and random. I would ask her about hooking up and say I was jacking off to her all the time, and she would say something personally spiteful. In brief moments of wispy humanity, we could talk about bird-watching or music, but then she would lash out erratically, so I would tell her she was being mean, which infuriated her even further. Then she said she would fuck me but we definitely could not be friends. I told her nice things only happen to nice people, which she spat back as coiling and uncoiling filaments of tenderlessness. She was spending time at her parents' more often than not, which meant she was broke.

A couple weeks later, Moira wrote and asked if I'd gotten a package she sent, which made me nervous because she had never been to my house. I looked around and didn't see anything and asked her what address she'd sent it to. It was to some not-even-remotely-related street and number several blocks away. Then she wrote fifteen minutes later and said she tossed something over the gate into my yard. Now even more nervously, I went outside to look but again didn't see anything. She didn't ride the bus, didn't have a car, and didn't have a decent job, so she would've had to have taken a twenty-dollar cab ride to get to what she thought was my neighborhood, which for her would have been a lot of money.

I wondered if it was something harmless like a book or record I'd given her and if she just wanted to erase me from her room. Or maybe she'd thrown the strap we bought onto an old grandma's grass that she thought was mine. Or maybe it was a cruel, rambling letter about things I never did, or maybe it was an anthrax letter or a box of rotting human shit or my sister's chopped-off arm. When I told her there was nothing to be found and was trying to lighten things up, I teased her for surprising whoever ended up with whatever she had sent and personally delivered. This sent her on the most convoluted and insulting tirade yet. I told her to never contact me again. She sent me a chiding advice pamphlet about sexual addiction and I told her again to never contact me. She replied emphatically with the same. *Maybe* I was *addicted*, I thought for one second, and then just jerked off to her.

Six months passed, and I was bored in an apartment in Switzerland where, due to poor planning, I had been alone for three days, waiting for the rest of an art group I worked with to arrive. I drank a bottle and half of not-great wine and every ten minutes sent Moira maybe-funny or peculiar but innocuous photos of plants or air-raid sirens until I got to magic number seven. After my mind cleared a little, I wrote and said I was drunk and jet-lagged and had no excuse and was sorry for bugging her. I said that I apparently must be missing her and that I hoped she was A-OK. She wrote a day later but quite late at night in her time zone, saying, "I am in the boonies at my parents'. I am fine."

I waited an hour to try and be cool and wrote, "How is it? What's new?"

She did not reply. I have no expectation that she will and every expectation that I will wish she would.

THREE THREESOMES,
NONE OF THEM GREAT

By determination, alcohol, and luck, I have had eleven or twelve threesomes. Even the best one, though, would only be rated six out of ten magenta stars. The median hovers around a soft two point five. For all involved, it would seem like when there are more holes, it should be better than this. The conspicuousness of my being the common denominator of these low scores is not lost on me. It only happened once, but I would like to state for the record that the highest score belongs to two of my former across-the-street neighbors, a middle-aged couple with three kids who likes to pretend to be—wait for it—elves. Talking dirty, double goo-ing, and double pissing in high elfin voices, all while wearing green felt elfin caps. They asked that I talk in my normal human voice, but believe me, I would have talked like an elf if they wanted me to.

One day, there was an envelope under my doormat, and in it was a photo of a woman from behind, bent over and grabbing her ankles, with my first name written across her ass. Her face wasn't visible, but there was a phone number. Normally, someone I didn't know leaving something at the door would concern me, but naked photos go a long way toward disintegrating the wary cautions of dedicated adult masturbators. I threw a towel across the kitchen counter and got to work.

We started to talk, and she left me a couple other obscured photos but also left distinct and even more pointed requests to bang. I showed them to Lana, and she said the photos being hard to make out could either be because the woman in them, whose name was Ana Paula, wanted—not unreasonably—to maintain anonymity, or else she was a beast. We both wanted a threesome, though, and Ana Paula talked a nasty enough game over the phone, so whatever. We set a date at a fancy hotel.

We met in the lobby, and Lana and I did everything we could not to shoot each other a look because Ana Paula was—there's no way around it—pretty unattractive. She was not grotesque, which might at least have been an experience, but she was well away from what even the kindliest of WASP relatives would call plain. Her whole thing was pastured in carelessness, bad skin, and underwhelmingly kooky tattoos. She was also wearing abnormal, unflatteringly fitted clothes that set her first impression in the off-puttingly grouped colors of ochre, pea green, electric neon blue, and umber.

One of the first things she said when we sat down for necessary drinks was that there was a sculpture near the entrance of the Los Angeles Central Library that she had posed for as a little girl. We both knew which one she was talking about and now had the joyful image of her as a child to contend with as well.

Lana said she had left her wallet in the car, and I told her I would walk her out to get it.

"Well . . ."

"Yes, unclear photos for a reason."

"What do you think? I could easily leave right now if you want."

"No . . . we might as well?"

When we returned, it was obvious Ana Paula knew what was discussed. We didn't want her to feel bad, so we immediately ordered more drinks, kept chatting, and then up we headed to our room. In the elevator, Ana Paula said she had gotten her own room, too, so we could play in one and then sleep in the other and get breakfast together in the morning. The total prick in me thought she was being a little hopeful.

Lana drank some more, which I knew she needed to do if this was going to happen. Ana Paula took out a joint and they split that too. I got all uptight about paying a fee for smoking in the room, but they paid no attention. Then we got in a circle and started to kiss. Right away, I thought, *Hey, she's good at this*, and, *Crisis averted!* We took our clothes off and the crisis was reasserted by her overwashed, sagging Walgreens panties with a hole in them and her remarkably asymmetrical breasts. They were of such different sizes and so malformed that I had to choose to think *interesting* rather than *disorienting*. It was like a kumquat next to a sweet potato. But then Ana Paula went down on me and I was impressed; her skills redeemed the night. Lana, now high as fuck, did not seem to care about anything anymore and was going for it.

For about half an hour, things were cruising along nicely and I thought that it could be really cool to have this be a regular trio if we were all into it. Then Ana Paula said she wanted me to fuck her in the ass. I asked her if she wanted to get fucked in the pussy and the ass and she said that I would have to be sure to wash myself really carefully. I said that I meant that Lana could wear a strap-on and we could DP her. Ana Paula's eyes turned to sparkles, and she stuck out her tongue to pant and say yes and yes over and over.

Lana showed her the toys she'd brought and Ana Paula picked a pretty thick black peg. Lana strapped it on and sat on a big, puffy chair. Ana Paula straddled her and slid it in. I got behind her and started the usual twenty-minute pre-anal ritual, but she reached back, grabbed my hips, and shoved me right in. Again, impressive. She fox howled like a champ. I could feel the toy against my cock through her body, and three became one. Ana Paula worked it pretty deeply for a long and hot time and then told me to cum in her ass. She was almost fiendishly into it. I kissed her all over her ass cheeks and went to shower and clean up.

When I came back, Lana was tied up and on the bed. She dug this kind of thing, but Ana Paula was hitting her with a whip incredibly hard. I could see Lana squirming in a way that made it clear to me that it hurt too much. To try and slow things down, I started to mess around with Lana, kind of making a barrier of friendliness between them. Ana Paula whipped my side and I gasped, "Too hard, too hard!"

Then she hit me again and I tried to laugh it off to keep from things getting out of control. The feel in the room palpably went from jackpot to disquiet. Lana said she wanted Ana Paula to watch the two of us mess around and jerk herself off. I think we were both giving her the benefit of the doubt that maybe she'd just never whipped anyone before and didn't know how to do it.

I started to spank and throw Lana around in the way that she liked, I guess kind of to show Ana Paula how to do it. She got impatient and made a shitty face. After a minute of what was starting to get intense and hot between Lana and me, Ana Paula pushed me out of the way and trumpeted that it was time for me to get spanked. All at once, there were no directions home.

My bottom days with women were pretty well over, but considering what a generous maestro she was at DP, I figured I had better do it. She left Lana tied up. I lay down on my stomach and she started to whack me with her palm. It was still too hard and I tried to say, in the least boner-killing way possible, that it could ease up a little. But then she, with no lube and no warning, jammed two fingers and two long, jagged fingernails up my ass. I like stuff up there, but I have to go very, very slowly. There was a white flash of pain, and the first thought I had was that I was really glad I was not tied up. Filled with the perishing spirit, I shouted and jumped up.

It was obvious now that Ana Paula was way higher than I realized because she barely reacted to any of this, beyond looking impatient. She started to bite Lana on the thighs while I tried to calmly untie her and not make things worse. I told her that I was pretty much done for the night and started to get dressed. Lana looked freaked out but was still real buzzed, so I got her clothes for her. While getting dressed, she came around and realized something was not right.

Ana Paula looked very confused and sat on the bed, saying she was really looking forward to cuddling in the other room and that she knew where I lived. I told her that sometimes

I get a little busted up and overemotional about sex and that Lana needed a ride home, so we were going to go. Ana Paula said in a whiny voice that we could just sleep here, but I told her *thank you for everything* and *sorry I'm being so brusque* and *please excuse that I'm nuts.* She started to stomp around the floor in a square dance of fits. We split and didn't say a word on the drive back.

When I got home, I couldn't sleep and got completely wasted and watched a bunch of movies. My ass was seeping and absolutely killing me. At the time, I lived in a bad neighborhood but, just as it was getting light out, I figured I could go for a little walk. I'd been sitting on a bag of ice and the water had soaked into my pants, but I left them on. Long ovals of someone else's not-dried blood were cast away on the sidewalk next to a scoop of human shit. There was an old woman being pushed in a wheelchair with her not-a-hallucination eyeball dangling out of the socket while she was screaming, "Faster, you faggot! Faster, you faggot!" at the almost equally worse-for-wear, neckless hulk behind her. I looked at the thickly-painted-in-frightening-red apartment doors that led to the doom flats above all the doom shops on Alvarado Street.

A few years later, I was at the Berlin Biennale to play a show curated by a friend of mine. The best after party was supposed to be at the Cameroon Pavilion. When I got there, it seemed like there were about fifty annoyed people from Cameroon and then, like, two hundred stoked white people from Europe. A troll-shaped woman with gnarled acne cornered me, speaking and walking like a replicant. I was down the bottle, so I was easy to corner. She said she knew an acquaintance of mine named Dubious Jørg who was at this party. He did performance art dressed like a purple goblin on Rollerblades and talked about the internet and annoying crap like that. He also had an unnecessarily obtuse haircut. They both had being annoying in common, and she whispered that they had slept together and that his dick was real big. Her name was Yo-Yo. We kept bumping into each other on the dance floor and at the bar, and she kept giving me inadvertently comical sex eyes.

Drinking never slowed, and as the party was ending, Yo-Yo and Jørg told me that they wanted to have a threesome. At the moment they finished saying this, my friend's way-too-skinny gallery manager stumbled over to me and started kissing my glasses. She told me to come to her room. I swayed around the unexpected options and told her that I had just been invited to a threesome and asked her if she wanted to come too. She tilted her head to the side and then asked who it was with, and when I told her, she laughed a loud, fake laugh and then walked away. Yo-Yo looked at me, so I shrugged and said, "Let's go."

There is a thing in some parts of Europe where you absolutely cannot bring a guest into your hotel room. The staff freaks out about it and loves to tell you no, especially if it's really late. I suspected this might be the case tonight but only had one key, so the obvious workaround wasn't an option. I gave it to Yo-Yo and told her to rush upstairs to my room like she belonged there, and Jørg and I would follow a minute later. She got in all right but made some noise, I guess, which alerted the night clerk, so he was looking around by the time we went in. He recognized me from before and said I could go

194

in but that under no circumstances could Jørg. It was about 4 a.m., and the night clerk looked like he was fifteen years old. We were wasted, so we just plowed past him while he screamed that he would call the police. We figured the police had more to do, so we weren't worried.

We knocked on the door and laughingly told Yo-Yo about our bullying past this kid, and then we started to make out. She had horrendous breath and pretty quickly we were all naked. Jørg's dick was bigger than average but not super giant, like Yo-Yo said. He was uncut and cleanly shaved and was passably good-looking, despite his art and haircut. Yo-Yo and I started to suck him off, then she said she wanted to suck both of us off. I stood and she put me in her mouth, but it was like putting my cock into a bank envelope of driveway gravel. Jørg seemed to be into it, but I couldn't deal with her harsh, chipped teeth, so I delicately pulled out and just watched them. She had a gross body, but hidden upon it somewhere were nice boobs.

Jørg sat on the bed with his back against the wall, and Yo-Yo reverse straddled him so I could see his cock go into her. I got in front of them and licked her clit and his rod while it went in and out. It was fun. Then he put on a condom, laid her down, and started to plow her alone. She was into it and was inspired to try and blow me again. I figured I should give peace a chance, so I put it in her mouth, but she just rampaged again and I lasted thirty seconds before it hurt too much. I settled for touching his ass and her tits while they went at it. Jørg kissed me a little and then asked to put it in my ass, but I wasn't really cleaned out and there was no lube around. He looked bugged by this.

They fucked for a while and then he pulled out, took off his condom, and then pushed back into her. She saw this but didn't seem to care. He started speeding up and saying, "Did you cum? Did you cum?" over and over.

She said, "Say it in Dutch! Say it in Dutch!" but he wouldn't do it.

There was a tremendous pounding on the door, and we all stopped dead. Being the least engaged, I got up to see what was going on through the peephole. It was the front desk child and two cops. The cops said through the door that my guest had to leave or we would both be arrested. Jørg started to curse loudly and Yo-Yo slid onto the floor to hide beside the bed. When I let them in, the night desk guy's arms were crossed and his little Sammy Hagar mustache looked extra satisfied. He had done his job. I tried to tell the anti-party time special forces to fuck off, but they were quite serious, so Jørg got half-dressed and stormed out. The desk guy looked at me and I slurringly asked him if he knew what *pedantic* meant. He turned red and left with the cops in a cloud of steam.

Yo-Yo climbed back onto the bed and said, "Let's go." She got onto her hands and knees to get done from behind. For the first time, I could see that her ass crack was hairy like a scarf an old yak might knit for another old yak and that she had pale, swinging hemorrhoids in a bunch of veiny, warm-colored grapes. I turned her over onto her back to avoid this disarray in missionary and we started. Her arms were lolling above her head and she was developing an eye-rolling, butcherly expression. It was maybe kind of hot but also kind of disturbing. I was getting close, and she told me to pull out

196

and shoot onto her chest. There had been a lot of buildup, so I could feel it was going to be good.

When I was there, I reared back and grabbed myself to jerk it, but she shouted, "Ho-ho," slapped my hand away, and grabbed my cock in both fists. She started pumping me but did it so tightly and so erratically that it just felt uncomfortable, and my jizz was wrecked. She looked at me like we were new parents and our beautiful daughter was my disappointing paste.

I lay down and thankfully passed out. When the sun woke me up a couple hours later, I had an unspeakable hangover. I was glad to see Yo-Yo was gone, but she had stolen a really nice wallet I'd bought for my brother-in-law. I knew that she stole it and that I didn't drunkenly misplace it because there was a note in the shopping bag it came in. It said, *Thanks for the wallet. Now forget all about my luving.* I had this note on my bulletin board for about a year because it *was* hilarious, but then I got mad about the wallet one day and threw the note down a storm drain.

A few nights after I got rid of that fucking note, Lana and I went to a literally-grimy-but-somehow-still-in-business-and-unchanged-since-the-late-1990s-style arcade. She had a steady girlfriend at this point, so we weren't really bonking anymore, but we were still totally friends—better friends, actually, since we didn't have to battle friends-with-benefits prudence anymore. We were quietly affectionate in public, so most people thought we were a regular couple.

She and I were playing *Time Crisis* and laughing and screaming when we noticed a woman in her late twenties standing behind us. We asked if she was waiting on the game and she said, "No, just watching . . . your asses." Lana and I looked at each other, raised our eyebrows, and unadvisedly—"Fuck it"—shrugged.

Her name was Amanda, and she said she was "living all about my own pleasure." She was on the cusp of not-all-that-cute if you looked at her one minute, and then the next minute she was almost pretty. We talked for a while, but she seemed too normal to me. Lana was more into her, but she was stoned. Amanda had moved to Los Angeles from South Carolina to work in theme park management and talked a lot. Post-Ana Paula, we decided not to rush into anything but wait a few days and see how it felt later. When I then asked Lana what she wanted to do, she said, "Eh, sure." I was still not super into Amanda, but I missed doing it with Lana, so it would be fine.

It took a long time for our schedules to line up and it wasn't until six weeks later that we got together, but the only slot that would work was on a Sunday between 11 a.m. and 3 p.m. All that weekend, Amanda was going to a super jive music festival but didn't like any of the bands that started before four o'clock. The only room I could find for those hours that wasn't basically an SRO was at a short-term airport hotel near LAX.

When Lana and I arrived, Amanda was in the lobby. The people at the desk looked us over smugly; they must've seen this setup all the time. Amanda looked a little worn-out. Her hair wasn't really combed and she was wearing baggy UCSC shorts but a UCSD tank top and very high grabber-green platform sandals. Her outfit, such as it was, had grass stains on the seat, and when I went to hug her, she stank of BO. This bummed me out, and it occurred to me that I hadn't paid for the room yet, so we could've jetted right then and gotten a burrito. Oddly, Lana didn't seem fazed and was being friendly and warm, which surprised me because she was really particular about hygiene. She was also exceedingly polite with people she didn't know well, though.

On the elevator ride up, we all seemed a little nervous, and I was still hoping someone would bail. The room was fine, and we sat on the bed and talked for a little bit. Then Lana and Amanda started to kiss. Amanda said she liked to be spanked and I knew Lana did, too, so I swatted them both while they took their shirts off. In theory, this should have blown my brains out, but Amanda smelled so bad that it was a lot to ignore. The going-way-too-far sandals were a nice touch, but that was the only nice touch. Lana was an ass queen and really wanted to lick and worship Amanda's ass in that special way, but I could see on her face that she wasn't that psyched about it when she pulled down her panties. Amanda's ass wasn't yucky, but it was neutral, as far as naked asses go.

They kept making out and I kept double spanking, but I wasn't getting turned on, and I hadn't noticed I was still fully dressed until they asked me if I was going to take any of my clothes off. As I was getting undressed, Lana started to go down on Amanda but then stopped abruptly and started coughing. I thought she just had something caught in her throat, but when I came over to join them, I saw that there was a thick, beige fudge all over Amanda's puss lips, hole, and little pubic tuft. It was rough. Lana, for some insane reason, gave it another go but then started full-on retching and got up to wash her mouth and face off. Amanda looked at me blankly. I had no idea what to do, but some innate adherence to social contracts pushed me forward and I started to suck her boobs. Adherence to innate biochemical contracts, however, categorically prevented me from getting my mouth anywhere near that sludge. She tried to guide me down there, but I held fast and she gave me a dirty look. *Fuck off* was my most present thought.

Somehow Lana rallied, and we all started to jerk each other off in a sluts' triangle of denial. Lana got out a pretty mighty dildo and started to slide it into Amanda, and I could see the cake collecting around it. Amanda put me in her mouth and gave pretty solid head, which felt super confusing. I absolutely did not want to fuck her but felt like I had to. I put on a condom and did my best. It did not feel good. Amanda lay there with her eyes closed and didn't seem real into it either. There were gobs of old deodorant falling out from her armpits onto the sheets. Lana put a vibrator on Amanda's clit while I fucked her, and I kept thinking about how spoiled all her toys were becoming. I looked over at Lana, who has an amazingly nice body and an immaculate pussy that tastes like candy, and I thought it might be my last chance to fuck her and what was I doing, wasting my life in the foul abyss.

I got up and went to the shower and scrubbed myself off for about seven hundred hours. When I got back, they were watching each other jerk off. Just as I got to the bed, Lana squirted all over me and started giggling about what she knew was a study in contrasts for me. I turned her over on all fours and we fucked. It was desperate and hot. This likely being our last time and doing it in the face of adversity made it feel like our village was being bombed by the Americans and we were teenagers in love. I forgot all about Amanda and shot cum in a high arc across the troublesome El Segundo afternoon sky, and it formed a beautiful, dear-hearted cloud. Jesus sat upon it, waving a streamer and smiling a little smile.

Lana immediately turned around to suck me hard again, and then I gave Amanda a few obligatory thrusts before I went permanently soft. She held the vibrator against her clit and came a small cum, then lay back on the bed, expressionless. I was significantly past ready to get the fuck out of there. When I got up, I was holding the dildos and other toys and Lana said, "Be sure to wash those." After another seven hundred hours of scrubbing, of which Amanda did not partake, liberty reigned and we all rode down the elevator together. She said she wished it had gone on longer and we didn't say anything.

In the parking lot, we gave her a very quick hug and waited for the valet to give us our keys, but he was organizing some visiting university's marching band and color guard, flags unfurled, into a livery of golf carts. It was funny. In the car, Lana and I looked around to make sure Amanda was gone and then started to scream, "EWWWWWW!!! EWWWWWWW!!! EWWWWWWW!!!"

We did go and get a burrito then. The food was unremarkable, but the brightly colored, brightly lit, family-style Mexican spot was amusingly surreal after what we'd just done.

"Why? Why!"

"I don't want to talk about it ever again. I may be ruined for snatch forever."

"Should we call her or something tomorrow?"

"Fuck no!"

About a week later, Lana and I went to get a shave ice. We hadn't talked at all in the meantime, which was unusual for us. She handed me a paper bag with a pair of her panties in it. I gave her a cockeyed look and she told me to smell them. I did, and it was like a felony of decayed mayonnaise and ham. She said that her cunt smelled like this now and that Amanda had given her some kind of infection. The doctor said it would take about three weeks to go away and that her girlfriend refused to fuck her now and she was afraid they would probably break up. After months of back and forth, they ultimately stayed together and, although eternally rooting for Lana's happiness, I was privately disappointed.

MARK WEST

A friend and I were playing a show together in Brussels. She brought along a person named Mark to do a simple but unusually curious projection show during her set. Usually, I think that if you need some kind of visuals to keep things going musically, then you should just practice more instead. In this case, though, the lighted images were creative and subtle and were neither jive nor a crutch.

After the show, Mark and I were making out while I should have been helping pack up. All we were doing was a little groping, but I felt Mark's cock on my stomach. It was so big that it poked up well over the waistband of his pants. It was like a feat of strength. I was dying to touch it or say something but just kept trying to look down while we were kissing in the dark. He wanted to do more but it was in the early days of touring, when the band I play in put up with booking agents giving us thirteen-hour drives between shows, so I had to get going.

Five years later, my friend had a little hit and we were playing together again at the same venue, but this time it was packed. I saw Mark, who now lived in Brussels, on the stage when we arrived. He was setting up the same light show as last time. I walked up and, in front of everyone, asked if we were going to make out again. He laughed and kept doing what he was doing. He looked good, better, five years older.

Before we were going to play, I was in the dressing room, taking a little snooze, and Mark walked in. He unbuttoned my pants and started spitting on my cock from an arm's length. The act of spitting seemed to turn him on. Then he put me in his mouth. With all the spit everywhere, it looked yucky but felt great. Someone knocked on the door to drop off dinner and Mark kept sucking away. The delivery person said, "Cheers!" and left. Mark gave me a wink and said he had to go too. I worthlessly tried to return to the nap.

After the show, there was a party, but I just wanted to go to sleep. I asked Mark if he wanted to come to the hotel with me. The friend I played with told me to be careful with him, thinking that Mark and I were about to bang. I took it to mean that I should treat him kindly. Mark said he was drinking with people and seemed sheepishly hesitant, so I gave him a peck on the cheek and split. When I got to my unusually nice room about twenty minutes later, the first thing I did was throw off my clothes off and start to jack it.

My phone rang and it was Mark, saying he was downstairs. One part of me just wanted to cum, take a shower, and hug my pillow to death. But since he showed up only a couple of minutes after I got there, he more or less must have followed me, and I didn't want to be a drag. I put my clothes back on to go get him. The lobby featured a remarkably good Billy Joel impersonator playing piano. My dad worked with Billy Joel when I was a kid and he used to come to our house to play handball against the garage door.

In the elevator, Mark stank of well drinks but seemed to be holding his booze all right. When we got to the room, he spread himself all over the bed. I asked him if he wanted to take a shower and he said no. I wanted him to because he smelled so strongly, but I couldn't really say that. I sweat like a disgusting hippopotamus during shows, so I took one. He looked in through the steam once or twice, which I thought was cute.

When I got out, I tried to look sexy with a towel wrapped around my waist. Mark looked me up and down and said he wanted to put it in my ass. He pushed me against the wall and alternated between stuffing his tongue up my hole and then spitting on it from a distance like he had with my cock. I usually like to top younger guys, but he was making this happen. He slapped my ass again and again while his face was inside it. I told him I wanted to look at his cock, mostly to see if I felt like it would fit, but he just said, "Get in line." It was terrifying.

He bent me over in half onto the bed, unzipped his pants, and poured a bottle of oil, which he took from his breast pocket, up my spread ass. It was warm and it made me feel open and a little more ready. I kept trying to look over my shoulder to see what was coming, but he was pushing on the back of my head to steady himself. His cock grazed my thighs and I could tell that it was going to be too big. My heart stopped, and I could feel a loud popping sound. He shoved it in me fast and severely, and I understood that the popping sound was a brief rip in the fabric of space and time presaging the fast and severe rip he had forced open inside of me. I never really healed correctly and can only take small things now, like one or two fingers at the most.

I flattened myself onto the bed and felt him pull out. There was blood and hurting everywhere on the white duvet. He was not wearing a condom. His cock was at least ten inches long and thick like a can of Red Bull. I got up and went into the shower again.

I stayed under the hot water a long time, hoping so much that he wouldn't be there when I got out. I watched bloody water pool classically around my feet and then watched it wash away. When I was done, he was in bed on the side with no blood, asleep. I got under the sheet and he started to snore. The sound was like a construction worker beating an elephant seal. I looked at his closed eyes, picked up the receiver of the hotel phone, and smashed him in the face with it as hard as I could again and again until he left. He never said *Stop* or asked *What are you doing?*

GLORY HOLE

At the office of a vanity magazine in San Francisco, I was doing an interview based on a collection of Polaroids our tour manager, Crayola, had taken while we were anywhere but at shows. The woman conducting the interview was a friend of his. The first time we talked was while the band was on a long drive through Nevada to California and we were amazingly tired of going somewhere. To scoot malaise along, we were calling everyone we knew and making them listen to our inconsequentialities.

Among these people was this music writer; her name was Eunice and she spoke German to us the entire time. It was silly but good. Along with Crayola, I met her and other friends of his in person for the first time a few days later in a grocery store parking lot. She fed me ice cream with a spoon and made fun of me while sitting on the bumper of my mini-van. A week later, she called to do this interview.

When I got to the office, which was decorated by Americans trying to impress Italians, she took me by the wrist into a kind of eternal foyer with a hundred low white couches along the walls. I hadn't gotten this when we first met, but there was something about the way she smelled or some other sybaritic chemical influence that immediately and vibratingly turned me on. I have never experienced this sensation as potently or as ferally as I did with her that afternoon.

We sat, and she would show me one of the Polaroids and ask for a quote to print as a caption. The initial ones I gave were just descriptions of what was in the pictures. Eunice told me she thought I had an imagination, which made me laugh, so instead I recited little non sequitur rhyming couplets for them. She seemed much happier with this.

We finished up pretty quickly. Even though she wasn't being excessively flirty, she was being playful, and like anyone shy, any attention I don't have to work for cranks me up. I crossed my legs to smush away my there's-just-something-about-her erection. She took me to a falafel place I hadn't been to in forever but used to go to all the time. It was nice to be there again, and I tried to impress her with my former connection. She was unimpressed by my falafel experiences but was still being nice and friendly and still laughing easily. I was hooked but of inferior wit and knew nothing would happen.

Eunice had very big boobs and was wearing a tank top. I had to concentrate not to stare but would cretinously glance down every little bit, hoping she wouldn't notice. When she got up to pay the bill, I watched her ass, which was like a piece of paper. She was wearing tight pants and it was legs, a flat plane, and then her back. I wanted to use her ass as a desk and pretend to be her assistant, signing her duplicate work orders in red and blue pencil while she took a boss's nap. As we were walking out, I asked her if she needed a ride, but she told me she biked everywhere, which made me love her piece of paper even more because it was a powered-by-muscle piece of paper. I very self-consciously tried to just shake her hand as we left, but she gave me an appropriate one-second, one-arm half hug. Even this little bit of contact made me want to cum to blot out the sky.

When I got into my now-historic minivan, I was hammer punching my cock and balls over my pants and thinking I would have to rub one out right that second or I would die. A cop drove by and I stopped. I had parked on a kind of chancy block that was all sex-worker hotels and adult toy stores. Through the windshield, I saw a sign that said VIDEO ARCADE and got out of the car and booked over to it.

It was called Adult World and was a legitimate Peter Sotos detention center. The walls, counters, floor, and display cases, such as they were, appeared to have been made of old cardboard boxes. The guy by the door was wearing thick glasses and stank, and he was sitting and wriggling on the heap of children he pedophile-murdered like Smaug upon his gold. In the back, faithfully, was the arcade. If you've never been to a "jack shack," it's a hallway with little plywood booths in a row that feature four video monitors you can toggle through to choose which pornos you want playing. You put in money, lock or don't lock the door, and then jerk it onto the floor. Sometimes there's a dark window between booths so that if both people turn on the light, you can watch each other pull it. The booth I went into had a splintery glory hole that had been chewed out by rats centuries before.

I put in five dollars and scrolled through the choices, looking for anyone with huge boobs and no ass. At my hip I heard a little whimper: there was the Mouth chirping at me. Its lips were incredibly swollen, cracked, and whitely moist. It was surrounded by a wire mustache and green plastic scrubber beard. The sounds it made were not words. I looked for any Eunices and got hard.

The Mouth started making sucking sounds and I shoved my dick into it. The Mouth, also known as No-Hands Merlin, had a condom inside it already and eloquently wrapped me up. Settling on a movie-version Eunice, I let the Mouth take me on. It was practiced and very hungry. Being super aroused before I arrived, I was ready to burst. Getting a blow job with a condom can be a lot of work, but the Mouth was pretty good at it. As a pixel, Eunice was squirting and exploring her own nipples with a long tongue. I scooped myself out of the Mouth, took off the condom, and yanked out a stream. In a man's trying-to-blubber-like-a-little-girl voice, the Mouth squeaked, "No! No! Mine! Mine!" and put its eye up to the hole to watch. The Tongue then started shooting in and out of the rat hole with mechanical licking jabs and the entitled, frustrated snorts of a mugged-for-nut casualty. Before I had my pants up, it disappeared, and the door next to mine opened and closed. I heard a scurrying sound and wondered if the Mouth would be out there. Would we meet? Should we bow to one another? When I left, the hall was empty, except for the haggard dust devils of what it meant for us to be garbage.

XXL

Occasionally, I play in an Italian psych band called XXL. Everyone in it is a beautiful and genuine supreme. We were on a tour and had a day off after a show in London. The drummer, an abyssal fuck machine handsome enough to pull as much dick as he wants, mentioned a gay sex club he'd heard of, fatedly also called XXL. I said, "Go, go, go!" The whole band, our tour manager, and a couple of friends spent the day at museums, drinking cider, eating Indian food, taking a million buses around the town, and then going to an absinthe bar. It was already a super-fun day and was quite late by the time he and I left to go all the way out.

The taxi driver seemed to know what the club was about and kept giving us knowing looks. When we arrived, the drummer and I went our separate ways after a small hug. At one point, I saw him squatting on his haunches with an enormous shaft in his mouth. I gave him the GOOOOOOAL sign. He somehow managed to laugh a little and shot me a wink, which pinged around the high arches of the club like a bouncy diamond. Other than that, though, I didn't see him the rest of the night, and I don't think we took the same cab back to where we were staying.

The place was normally a giant dance club, so the main rooms looked like discos. A lot of people were, in fact, just dancing, and like at all gay dance clubs, no one paid attention to me. I encouragingly reminded myself that forlorn dancing was not what I came here for. On the patio was a post-junk, post-too-much-Thailand-vacation-but-trying-now-and-on-a-health-kick-looking guy reclined in a fuck sling. He might have been thirty or he might have been fifty. His hair was a sandy bowl.

He whistled as I walked by and, still feeling the requisite, tedious sting of the dance floor, I turned. There were some empty poppers on the ground under him and a tub of ass lube on a stool next to him. He looked too strange to fuck, but I wondered if I could try and fist him. I put a rubber on my finger and slid it in his loose butthole. It was like a hot dog in a hallway. I gave him the *Want another?* look and slid a second one in. My fingers walked with their arms around each other along the beach until they came to a cute little grass hut whose proprietor was selling tropical rum coconut drinks.

He started to squirm and moan. It felt like the poppers must be wearing off or else he had an Incredible Hulk's O ring. My fingers were squeezed tight-tight as I slid in and out. He started reacting like an electric eel. It was not like human enjoyment. He panted, "Stop, stop, stop." He was smiling, though, so I gave him a little kiss on the ear and resumed the quest.

So far, I did not feel great about myself. Naturally, I saw the entrance to the "dark room" and went in. I had never been in one before and imagined it would be a sandwich of love, one below and one above. Mostly, people were just moving around like in a circle pit, some touching but nothing too

212

full-on. Also, from what I could see, everyone was a Grimm's fairy tale and counting on the dark room being very dark.

A wheezing, dirty orb of hanging, disheveled teeth touched my arm and pulled out his tiny geometric dick. With no thought and no feeling, I started to jerk it for him. He put his waggling, slack arm around my waist and pulled me closer. He was sitting on a bench and wearing a mashed-up prisoner's cap and collarless smock. I stooped over a little to get at him. He didn't look at me, but I wanted to look at him. His face, even in the dim light, looked scabby and pitted by meteorites and space trash. His long, thin hair was like refrigerated grease spaghetti. Maybe he was nice to his pet turtles? His eyes followed the swirl of men around the room and his endless hips started to buck. Sometimes I don't want any disaster glop on me, so I disappeared.

There was a room of baroque couches no one seemed to be in, so I took a little soul's break and lay across one. I heard a trumpet's call to arms, and out of a bright lavender door on the other side of the room emerged a group of men, all of whom appeared to be at least seven or eight feet tall. I stood to see better. They were all in half uniforms of leather pants with leather suspenders, naked to the waist, wearing bondage ring belts and leather work boots. The group barreled toward me, staring menacingly over my head, and I had to jump out of the way to avoid being flattened. I wanted them to see me standing in their path, but they would not.

I returned briefly to a no-one sofa again to consider being further dispirited, but it was getting late, so I rallied and started to wander around. More and more men were doing it all over the place. It was pretty interesting. A guy—older than me, fit but not overly so, with short hair and a sweet, roughened face—walked over to me and smiled. Thank God. He told me his name was Yuri. He seemed to have a hard time pronouncing my name but tried anyway. We started to kiss and it was good. I got on my knees, untucked his dress shirt, and put him in my mouth. His cock was a good size for me, too, solid and handsome. After not very long, he moved my head away and stood me up. I was always worried that I was shitty at giving head, but I didn't want to wreck things and be pouty. I put my arms around him from behind, pressed myself against his muscled back, and put my cheek against his neck. It was fantastic.

He wrapped his hand around it and jerked until he came. It felt good feeling his arms and shoulders flexing as he shot. He turned around and I squeezed his balls to make him grin and shudder. We kissed some more, but then he started to cry. Yuri told me he had to come to London every two weeks for work from a city in Russia he was sure I hadn't heard of. He was never in either place long enough to get a relationship going, and this was the first time anyone had touched him in over a year. I gave him what I think was a real hug and he cried and cried. It should have been uncomfortable, but it was all right.

We talked a little more, but I had been at the club for long enough and felt ready to leave. He asked me several times for my number, but I said I lived too far away and would never see him. He asked for my email, but I told him I wasn't really wanting to start anything. He was sad about this, but I overripely told him I would make him sadder.

It was light by the time I got back. I called my best friend and talked to her about everything that had happened.

LEO CRAYOLA

Sometimes on tour, your brain and heart become completely filled with the creamed corn of feeling like a failure from being in gross bathrooms every day, from actually being a failure, and then forgetting the universality of how, where, and why? Everything is funny and nothing is fun. Due to the exhaustion of disappointment and the relentlessly fierce mix of emotions, it takes in between nine to fifteen days for inevitable "Tour Crazy" to set in. During our sixth year on the road, we had gotten into the habit of eating handfuls of coffee beans and, in a fit of exhausted hysteria, our tour manager, Crayola, poured an enormous bag of them all over the dashboard of the rental van. To our surprise and delight, they vibrated and slid down and into the defrost vent like pachinko balls. When we turned on the defrost fan, they shot out as a chorus into the air and all over the front seats. We laughed so hard and so maniacally, we almost crashed and had to pull over to catch our breaths and collect ourselves. For the rest of the tour, every time we turned on the vent, a few would pop out like little brown friends hailing fellows well met. The van smelled amazingly good.

I have seen lots of tour managers for other bands become disinterested, sagging pains in the ass after a while, but

Crayola would make up photo projects, organize art gallery and nature trips, and, most importantly, wildly encourage and foment chaotic behavior and unnecessary aesthetic mischief. He did not in any way try to manage nor corral this Tour Crazy.

We were sharing a 1960s misfortune motel in Tucson. It was Robin, Faven, Crayola, and me. Crayola was walking around the room in circles, singing over and over in a high, eldritch voice, "Pacific Ocean, sexy Pacific Ocean." He was holding a harp seal hand puppet we had named VuVu and whenever he sang "sexy Pacific Ocean," he would rub VuVu all over his chest.

After a thousand repetitions of the chant, Faven said, "Just go jerk off and shut up."

I said, "If you can jerk it all the way and spurt onto Faven's stomach in under twelve minutes, I will give you five hundred dollars each." We were paid in cash every night, so each of us had dummy wasting-money floating around all the time.

Robin laughed and said, "Being dead isn't being alive."

Faven said, "Fuck that. I want to see if he can do it."

We turned on the clock radio to a classical station at 12:15 a.m. Crayola took off his shirt, got on his hands and knees, and pulled down his pants. Faven lay down on a couch and raised up their shirt to show their stomach. Opening a beer and cupping their pudge into a malignant cinnamon's bun, they challengingly looked Crayola dead in the eye. He went to work.

After eight minutes, he had yet to achieve an erection. It is very difficult to jack off as a joke. He and I threatened to cum on each other's faces while we were asleep all the time but, despite our loving efforts, neither of us could even get close to pulling it off.

Faven began to berate Crayola in a baby-talk voice, "Am I too gross for you to get a boner? Am I really so disgusting you can't even get hard? Your dick is a fucking tragedy *and* a fucking comedy!"

This worked, and Crayola finally got it up. Everyone took a peek and murmurs of, "Oh, that's a healthy dick . . . " etc. went around the room. He had three minutes left to finish, and I reminded them that it was twelve minutes or nothing. He was furiously whacking and furiously whacking some more while Faven, still reclined with their tummy out, continued to hassle him.

"Blood is dripping out of your dick. I can taste your bloody cum in my fucking beer and it tastes like your bullshit girlfriend's asshole tampon!"

We lost track of time and it was 12:29. I made a game-show buzzer sound to let them know it was over, but he kept going and Faven kept reprimanding him. Fifteen more minutes passed. At this point, Robin was reading, I was reading, and Faven was still in position but was now also reading. They would occasionally say things like, "Who would you rather fuck, your mom or your dad?" but they were distracted by their book. Crayola was panting and still jamming his fist in and out of hope. A couple more times, I reminded them both that the bet was off and that I wasn't going to pay them. After ten more minutes, the radio was still playing classical music. Faven occasionally looked up to see how Crayola was doing, but they were over it. I think Robin might have forgotten it was still happening. Other than the radio and Crayola's breath, it was quiet.

"UUUUUH! I did it," Crayola said in a barnyard grunt. Robin and I looked up. Faven was somehow wearing sunglasses now and pointed at the jizz on their hairless stomach with a cocked finger and a homicidal sneer. They both wanted their money.

"I told you, like, twenty times it was off."

"I hate you! You piece of shit liar!"

"I said so many times I wasn't going to pay you guys anymore! Twelve minutes! Twelve minutes!"

"Fucking liar cheater!"

Robin got up and civilly handed Faven a wet towel, but something in the room had cracked open. Faven had twenty-three more beers left from a twenty-four-pack they'd lifted from the backstage. They started shaking them up and throwing the full cans at me. There were two ice buckets in the room. Crayola filled them both up over and over with hot water from the shower and started pouring them out onto the beds. Robin lifted the soaking mattresses up and barricaded the door with them. Then she crossed her eyes, growled, and purposely fell backward onto the air conditioner sticking out of the window. She is pretty tall and muscular, so it smashed out of the wall and onto the ground. I started to hurl myself against the waterlogged mattress fort. Gray sloshes of wet, depressing sleep were spurted onto the revolted carpet. Eventually, Innyhal, infernal spirit of Mars, felt his diabolical work complete, and we passed out.

A couple weeks later, we played an early show in Minneapolis, and the next day we had off. We were in the hotel by 8 p.m. and could sleep in, which meant drinking was more on than usual. After the show, we stopped by a gas station. I bought four dozen donuts and twelve assorted malt liquor forties. It was so much bad-for-you that I had to carry it all back in a huge box. Crayola had a friend in town named Chhorvin, and she followed us in her car to the hotel to hang out.

Minneapolis is a hard show to make. The place we play is always an early show and we need to get there by three instead of the usual six for sound check. Chicago is the day before but, conversely, that's always a late show. The venues are about six and a half hours apart. That means almost no sleep.

We were deranged by the time we lugged our stuff into the suite. The five of us stood in a circle, facing each other, and touched our forties together in another pentagram of *Fuck it*.

Robin and Faven went into one room and closed the door to do coke and talk to their sweethearts on the phone, so I lost touch with them. Crayola and I started to pound donuts with the malt liquor and felt yucky and screwy right away. There was a gym in the hotel and we thought we could try to walk it off and start over. Chhorvin came with us. We got onto treadmills and pressed start. In a minute, Crayola, whose feet were always a wreck, was limping and went back to the room.

Chhorvin was quite petite, and I asked her to climb on my back so I could give her an R. Crumb piggyback ride while I walked on the treadmill. She climbed on. I was already so jacked on sugar and booze that I could hardly feel her weight. She slid her hand down into the back of my pants, spread my

219

cheeks apart with two fingers, and started poking my butthole with the other finger. It felt really good but was clearly meant as a joke, and we were both cracking up. After a bit, someone came into the gym and she jumped off, wiped her finger on my hair, and we went back to the room.

When I opened the door, Crayola took off my belt, put it around my neck, and tried to put a sandwich bag over my head. It wasn't big enough to fit over my face, so it just sat on my head as a destitution miter. We took out a couple donuts and started to iron them on an ironing board. They were warm and flat and reeked of yummy dementia. I decided, then, to iron all of the remaining donuts and take one bite from each of them. This would take a while. Every minute or so, Crayola or Chhorvin would yank the belt around my neck and throw me onto the bed, interrupting my work. The iron would clang to the floor, but the donuts were so sticky they never fell off the ironing board. The TV was never on. We felt unrestricted.

Crayola wanted to take over the ironing and biting the donuts. I bowed out, filled the bathtub, and got in. Every time Crayola finished flattening a donut, he would throw it in the water with me. Chhorvin came into the bathroom and sat on the toilet lid to talk and drink. She spit malt liquor into my face. This turned me on, and I rose naked and half-hard from the donut sea and asked her for a hug. She pointedly did not look at my lame dick and said, "You are a fucking mutt," pouring the rest of her forty into the bath. She left and came back and sat on the edge of the tub with a book, and we sat together in profane contemplation.

Crayola finished his donut chores and came into the bathroom with us. He pulled the plastic bag off of my head and half filled it with booze, then he took down his pants and pissed in it. Chhorvin said, "Close your eyes," and took the bag. We heard her pull down her pants and piss in it too. I bit a tiny hole in the corner of the bag and Crayola held it up over my mouth like Dionysus's fetid and foregone wineskin. Chhorvin squeezed the bag and I drank all their pee-pee and booze.

Crayola said he wanted to do something special and asked me to stand up and bend over. He put his finger down his throat and barfed on my ass cheeks. I sat back down into the tub filled with donuts, old water, alcohol, piss and throw up. We could not stop laughing.

I was so drunk by now that I was almost not awake. The bath was getting cold, but I couldn't make myself get out. Chhorvin said she was going to go sleep, got up, and turned invisible on a puffy chair. Crayola closed the bathroom door and whispered to me, "I can tell you have a crush on Chhorvin. You know I used to go out with her?" He took me by my wrist and then put a hunk of his own shit into my hand. The belt was still around my neck.

Mostly, I don't drink on tour anymore. It has nothing to do with regret. It's just easier to keep my vocals together for longer, and of course I feel less physically rotten every day. This makes being on tour much less eventful, possibly even *un*eventful. Tour Crazy still invites itself along, but it's more like a strong, deep hit of sativa instead of an endless supply of mephedrone.

This is embarrassing, and I would never ever publicly admit to feeling nostalgic for anything else, but—big sigh—I miss everything about the "old days" of idiotic idiocy and every pandemonic effort divined to bring to reality our reprobate and necessary/unnecessary conjurings. We still get out to nature when there's time or do a little sightseeing or whatever, and while that's really nice . . . it's nice.

Aside from playing music, being on tour is pretty dull now. People always ask *what's the craziest thing that happened on your last tour* and all I can say now is something like, "Oh, I saw a black-billed cuckoo."

TORINO GUY

At first by chance and now by habit, I have spent a lot of time in Torino. It is the fabled resting place for the shroud of Turin and therefore also the geographic center of Satanism in Italy. I have some very close and dear friends there and never get tired of them, the chocolate, the food, or the Consolata.

We all eat at the same restaurant a lot, and when I ask my friends where we're going, they just say, "Oh, you know, that spot," and then I do know. There's a waiter there who I think might be the most handsome man I have ever seen. He is about five-foot-eight with a tight, salt-and-pepper haircut, and is lightly tanned and in shape. He is probably eight years older than me; has quick, darting, granite eyes; and a quick, darting, granite jaw. With a single glance, he transformed me into an exclusive fan of older guys. Now that I, too, am on or more likely past the cusp of being an older guy, I'm not sure how long I'll be able to keep that silver-laden boat afloat. BINGO BONGO!

Someone told me that he dated this other person in town who looked like and has the physique of, without any exaggeration, an ogre. I can't remember his name; maybe it was Gorgorax. He was real tall and had a slight hunch, a magnificently large head, muscles like propane tanks, and an

223

expression of flowed-out lava on his face. I loved to think about Torino Guy getting his ass's future ridiculed by what had to have been a muffler of a dong. Also, Gorgorax was widely known to have fucked Jimmy Somerville, the diminutive lead singer of Bronski Beat. Likewise, a remarkable image.

The friend I usually stay with in Torino runs a magazine and design firm. They were having a work party for its staff and people in the neighborhood "scene," and he asked me if I would sing a couple songs. Playing at work parties is a more than dumpy nightmare if you sing depressing, quiet, and dumpy songs, and that's all I had to sing. The sound systems always suck at these things and people talk through it because they're annoyed they have to pretend to pay attention to something they could not give a fuck about. It is basically torturing yourself and everyone else there for not enough money.

After I sang for twenty minutes and everyone hating it, I got a bottle of some booze or other and lay under a gigantic desk. I drank it very, very quickly and then felt less humiliated. While I was under there, a woman who was drunker than me crawled in too. She didn't notice me at first. Otherwise dressed normally, she was wearing orange rubber dishwashing gloves. When she finally realized she was not alone, she started to kiss me, but it tasted like barf. When I moved away, she put the dishwashing gloves on my hands and fell asleep. I squished out from under the desk to find some more booze.

I was in Torino then, working on a record, and one of the guys who was playing on it was insanely cute. We had been

224

holding hands a little and hugging more than friends do, but he was out of my league. The office party dance floor was at full-on blast, and one of my bandmates asked why I wasn't going for him and pushed us together. We danced for about thirty seconds, and then he took me by the wrist into a hallway and we started to make out. He was *de-vine*!

After a little bit, he said, "I'm really sorry, but kissing you is like kissing my brother." Sometimes he and I are still affectionate, but in an unfortunate, brother-cake sort of way. In the back office where we'd kissed was a huge, foam rubber block of prop cheese that the firm must have used for a photo shoot. It was at least four feet high, six feet long, and bright orange. I still had the rubber gloves on and made myself drunk-laugh by watching my hands disappear against it. I was wearing red pants and a pink shirt, so the colors looked super funny together. I climbed up on the cheese block and lay down. Then I closed my eyes and listened to the music from the other room.

The block of fake cheese started to wobble. It was Torino Guy. He roughly and fabulously yanked me off the block and into an alley alongside the building. He bit my neck hard, and it was as if all the sex I had ever had was annulled by his court. Thick hands on my shoulders, he pushed me onto my knees and undid his pants with one movement. He wrapped his calloused palms around my head and began to fuck my mouth, wildly looking left and right. It was amazingly amazing. I didn't get a good look at his cock, but it felt manly.

After maybe a minute, he pushed me onto the ground into a puddle. He stomped away chuckling and didn't look back at all. My ass was wet in the dirty water. It was kind of hot to be cast away like this, but I've always wondered if he shoved me off because he figured I was beneath him, someone saw us, or he was for real just too high. I prefer, of course, to presume it was because I was beneath him.

I sat there for a little bit until I caught up with how nasty it was to be in that nasty water. When I stood up, I saw a maybe-fifteen-year-old Albanian sex worker in the alley. She was wearing almost nothing and staring at me.

M.G.S.

On November 13, 2002, my father killed himself. He may have actually died on the night of November 12, but my mom found his body on November 13. Her own mother had died only six months before. At the time, I was working at someplace called the Child Development Center. The students were mostly from families of migrant farmworkers, and all the kids were super poor. The facilities weren't very well taken care of, and the largely inexperienced staff largely sucked. Frequently, instead of cleaning up the stray cat shit in the yard, every couple of days people would just draw chalk barriers around the piles so no one would play near them. It was a difficult and taxing place to be employed and a difficult and taxing place to be a child.

I was commuting from Oakland four days a week, which was about a fifty-minute drive without traffic and an hour and a half with traffic. Usually, I took a nap in my van during my lunch break. An egg timer I'd stolen from the school's kitchen sat in the cupholder as an alarm clock. On the day of November 12, I was jolted awake by a lightning bolt. Beamed from God, there was a voice, clear as a bell: "Call your father right now."

His mental health had been deteriorating from years of drug abuse (mostly morphine and other prescription opiates),

227

unrelated manic depression, and perhaps—I never knew if this was true or not—a claim that one of the four doctors he was seeing stated that there was mold growing in his lungs. My mother told me he was seeing four doctors to get as many pills as he could, which is why it was hard to know what, if anything, was real. One day, he told me, "I don't want to work anymore," and then a month after that: mold. He sort of worked three days a week at home, two days at the office for a while, and then he stopped going in altogether.

At this time, he was working for Adobe, but instead of doing his job, he whittled away on a computer program of his own that, despite his explaining it to me, I couldn't really understand. He claimed it could monumentally and effectively improve the writing of computer code forever. My dad was an extraordinarily talented and intelligent person, so it wasn't implausible that perhaps he could have actually been in the midst of accomplishing this. He had invented other things, was a noted and gifted music arranger, and had produced a couple of huge pop and jazz records. I don't know for sure, but I think that this potentially magical, world-changing program, his last productive effort, was the beginning of him losing his mind. It was probably really just a drug-fueled, obsessive rabbit hole of numerology, graphics exploration, and a slow, concerted, self-induced rationalization of internal decay. This is hard for me to admit.

Once he stopped going to the office, he spent his time in bed and was unpleasant to be around. Occasionally he would slither from the depths up to the table at family dinners, say something aggressive or strange, and then go back to his room, keeping the lights out, looking at UFO shapes on his screen or making not-super-great artsy Photoshop collages of our family. I have one he did of me shooting quasars out of my palms against a galactic background while in a tai chi stance.

I didn't understand how far gone he was; I just thought he was being a pain in the ass. Once in a while, he seemed fine, so I chose not to see it. My sister had a baby around then, at which point my father, my sister's husband, my sister, their child, and my mom moved into my grandma's old house together. My father was nice with the baby, so I assumed things could not be so bad.

When he picked up the phone, I said, "Dad, I just wanted to tell you that I love you."

"No, you don't," he said.

There was the sound of weeping, and then he hung up. This was the last time we spoke. Since his decline, I had come to expect and then ignore comments like that from him. I decided to know that he knew I loved him.

He had been telling me for two years that he wanted to kill himself. It was more than I could process and I never told anyone. It was several years after his death that I mentioned to someone in my family that he'd been telling me this. When he did it, I wasn't surprised. I was relieved to not have to wonder when it would happen anymore and relieved that he was free from his suffering and that I was free from his suffering.

His parents were sensationally physically and mentally abusive, and his mind was plagued by mental illness and addiction. He had, at times, enjoyed great success but had, at times, been mightily fucked over in his professional life.

His health was bad and he had been falling apart from a youngish age due to a crap diet, drugs, not much exercise, and smoking—a body and mind that always hurt. As a child, I remember hearing his wailing cry from the shower and running outside to get away. He tried his best not to inflict the horrors of his childhood upon my brother, my sister, and me, and, unlike his own parents, he would tell us he loved us.

A lot of the time, he was stoned, absent, or a colossal and macho asshole, but considering the bucket of cement his feet had been born into, he'd made progress vis-à-vis us, I guess.

To have more time to work on music, I was trying to find a job with fewer hours and less stress than at that preschool, so I was applying to be a baggage handler for the Oakland airport. Everyone else there was massively tall and massively built. Through a cracked-open door around the corner of the dispatch place, I saw a warehouse of red dragon conveyor belts, immortal steam jets, and burly men singing in basso profundo about the legendary keepers of iron, mud, and coal. It felt unlikely that I could take the pace, but I didn't have a realistic life plan, then or now. After filling out my forms, I was told to go to a different office a couple of miles away for other paperwork.

On the freeway, I turned my phone on for the first time that day. I had taken to turning it off before bed because every night around 1 a.m., a bill collector would call for whoever used to have my number. There were twenty missed calls from my sister.

I called her back, and she asked if I was driving and said I should pull over. In that one second, the first thing that came to my mind was that her infant daughter had died. She sounded really shaken but was still making sense. Oddly, I thought, *Well, her daughter is so young, maybe she hasn't had enough time to really become attached, and so that's why she's not too upset.*

She said, "Dad is dead. Come home right now."

I turned my minivan around, left a frantic message on the voicemail of my work, and drove back to my place to get some clothes.

At this time, I lived in a warehouse apartment, and I have no idea why or how I lived there. It was worthless in every conceivable way. My roommate, Julio, was home when I got there, and I told him what had happened and that I would be gone for a week. He looked freaked out and gave his condolences. The walls were incredibly thin—just one panel of drywall that wasn't flush with the ceiling, and you could hear a page turn from the other side. Julio was super tall and had a super short girlfriend and I used to have to listen to them attempt anal a couple times a week. There would be a long crescendo of "Ow, ow, ow, ow, OW OW OW!" and then silence. Sometimes, to get back at them for being so loud, I would start jerking off while they fucked, which I could tell they heard because they would whisper about it and then stop what they were doing.

It took almost two hours to drive to my family's house in Sacramento. I don't remember what I thought about or felt on the drive, but when I pulled up, my mom was outside waiting for me. She looked like a zombie. I tried to make some small joke, which she would normally indulge, but she just wrapped her arms around me and we went inside.

This may not be entirely accurate—I've never asked exactly what the sequence of events was—but my understanding is that my dad had taken several dozen of a variety of opioids and high-dose antidepressants and then died during the night. My mother was sleeping in another room at the time and discovered him early in the morning. I suppose she then told my sister and her husband, who were also still living there. I don't know what my sister did; I really need to ask her. When a person dies, they usually void their bowels and bladder and, in this case, there were so many pills he also vomited. My brother-in-law cleaned up after him; I will forever be indebted to him for this. My mom worked at a funeral home and knew to call the coroner. When his remains were taken to the morgue, she also knew an autopsy would be performed, which is standard in suicides.

My mother told me that she'd thought something might have been wrong that day. She went to go get donuts from Krispy Kreme and asked my dad what kind he wanted. He blurted out, "All of them! Bring me all of them!" I can hear his crackling voice say this and it makes my stomach hurt. On September 6, 2001, I visited my brother in New York and we went up the Twin Towers, near the base of which there was a Krispy Kreme. A couple days later, it must have been smashed to dust.

I went into the bedroom where my dad died. It used to be my grandma's bedroom. On the mattress was a clean, white sheet. Dead center was a single, ghostly pill that appeared to be floating a centimeter above it. I asked my mom if it had been there before. She said it had not.

In that phantom's daze, I wandered into my dad's office, which was a mad-scientist laboratory. It used to be the spare room I would sleep in as a kid when I visited my grandparents. Once I let off a novelty store fart bomb in there and my grandparents locked me in to fully inhale it as punishment.

On top of my father's computer monitor was a copy of a record called *Chapel of the Chimes* by the band I'm in. He showed up to watch us play a couple of months before. It was the only time he ever saw us, and he was gracious, unusually lucid, and encouraging. During that show, I was playing a harmonium and someone from the nine-member audience asked me what it was. "Party Time," I replied, and I could hear my dad laugh. Now I have his exact same laugh, and sometimes when I'm alone and amused, I jump out of my skin when I hear him coming out of my mouth. There's a song on that record predicting my father's suicide from pills and disintegration. His copy of the CD was still in the shrink-wrap, but I was glad to see he had put it up. While I was looking at it, it fell to the messy floor as if knocked down by an unseen hand.

I found myself calling everyone I knew to tell them my father was dead. Most people didn't pick up the phone. I left a message for someone who I thought was my best friend but she never called me back. This revealed a lot to me about her, and I think I have never forgiven her for it. Someone who I was basically just using for sex called me over and over, but I didn't talk to her, maybe to have some control over anything.

My brother still lived in New York and got on the first flight he could. He arrived the next day. When you have a death in the family, you can get a discount on same- or next-day travel. He said that when our sister called him about our dad's death he started to throw up. He was at my mom's for three days before he learned it was suicide. Everyone assumed someone else had told him. He was shouting and angry for a moment, but then he calmed down and said he was glad that our dad had had some agency in his death and hadn't just faded out. Years later, he and I went to dinner to talk about it. He's always been emotionally distant, but he could barely contain himself. My brother now has two kids and says he could never imagine doing something like that to one's children, that he hates my dad and that he has no feelings anymore.

Each night until the funeral, my mom and I slept next to one another in the bed where he died. She and I didn't discuss it, but it seemed necessary. We all met at the funeral home where my mom worked to talk about the arrangements, which her colleagues would be taking care of. I kept trying to be funny, but people just stared at me or smiled painfully. My favorite joke of the day was referring to this event as DAD/11. I took a photo with my infant niece, dressed in black, sitting on Santa's lap during that week. It's on the back cover of a badly pressed LP reissue of a record we did called A Promise, the promise being that, for the sake of my mother, I would not kill myself. The title had been picked and the record finished a couple weeks before my dad bailed.

At the funeral, my uncle and his sons sang the Jimmy Cliff song, "I Can See Clearly Now." It will make me cry for the rest of my life when I hear it on the radio. My godmother told me that I looked like a businessman dressed in my suit.

I was asked to give the eulogy and I hardly kept it together while I was talking, but I muddled through. I'd written it out quickly in pencil right before the service. I now regret having mentioned in it that my childhood household was a difficult place to be; I noticed my mother nodding and looking away when I said it. I still have these pages in a drawer. One night, I must have drunkenly crumpled them up and then tried to smooth them out because I later found that they were wrinkled but flat.

There was an open casket and initially, I did not want to see the body, but after the service I went to say goodbye. He looked totally normal. Not even asleep—just normal, with his eyes closed. I put my hand on his chest, expecting to feel something, but it was like touching a cardboard box. There was NOTHING there. He was gone from that body and far, far, far away. In some ways, it was terrifying, and in some ways, I was glad to know he made it out. My godmother gave me a big hug after this.

My father had three or four children out of wedlock with women other than my mother. One of his sons came to the funeral. We looked at each other very closely in the eye and then embraced without saying anything. This was the only contact we ever had.

After the funeral, I gave my sister's friend Jason a ride home to San Francisco and then listened to a book on tape, *Lonesome Dove*. After I dropped him off, I drove all over Oakland trying to buy some porn magazines, but I couldn't find any.

For some reason, I don't think I drank a drop of booze that whole week. If it were now, I'm sure that is all I would have done.

Across from my apartment then was a temporary housing shelter. A man came up to me when I was getting out of the car and mumbled something. I gave him my black puffy coat, but I left my earmuffs in the pocket by accident. There were dozens of shooting stars that night, and the guy and I watched them together for a few minutes.

My father's remains were cremated. He had always asked that when he died, we mix some of his ashes in paint and, together as a family, paint this ash into a picture of a rhinoceros. My mother gathered us together at Christmas and, after pouring the remains from a Dixie cup, we swirled him into the colors and made the rhino. I added a little yellow bird to sit on its head.

The ash had chunks of bone in it, some about as big as a dime. I thought it would be like sand. I have a piece of his bone in a small cinnabar box, along with a lucky penny and a blue-green D&D die my brother gave me when we were children. I keep the die with the number three turned up—three for the Holy Trinity—and my father's bone is wrapped in tinfoil like drugs. Sometimes I take it out and stick it to the tip of my tongue.

ACKNOWLEDGMENTS

It has been a great honor, privilege, and surprise to have this book in the capable, generous, insightful, and most of all wildly accepting hands of Samuel Nicholson, Ian Bonaparte, Stefan Tobler, Tara Tobler, Tom Flynn, Nikita Zankar, Michael Watson, Emma Warhurst, Jeremy Davies, Larissa Melo Pienkowski, Tom Etherington, and Alex Billington. There are few other reasons to live than to have the opportunity to make something with such excellent people.

Dear readers,

As well as relying on bookshop sales, And Other Stories relies on subscriptions from people like you for many of our books, whose stories other publishers often consider too risky to take on.

Our subscribers don't just make the books physically happen. They also help us approach booksellers, because we can demonstrate that our books already have readers and fans. And they give us the security to publish in line with our values, which are collaborative, imaginative and 'shamelessly literary'.

All of our subscribers:

- receive a first-edition copy of each of the books they subscribe to
- are thanked by name at the end of our subscriber-supported books
- receive little extras from us by way of thank you, for example: postcards created by our authors

BECOME A SUBSCRIBER,
OR GIVE A SUBSCRIPTION TO A FRIEND

Visit andotherstories.org/subscriptions to help make our books happen. You can subscribe to books we're in the process of making. To purchase books we have already published, we urge you to support your local or favourite bookshop and order directly from them – the often unsung heroes of publishing.

OTHER WAYS TO GET INVOLVED

If you'd like to know about upcoming events and reading groups (our foreign-language reading groups help us choose books to publish, for example) you can:

- join our mailing list at: andotherstories.org
- follow us on Twitter: @andothertweets
- join us on Facebook: facebook.com/AndOtherStoriesBooks
- admire our books on Instagram: @andotherpics
- follow our blog: andotherstories.org/ampersand

CURRENT & UPCOMING BOOKS